SKIING

Developing Your Skill

SKIING

Developing Your Skill

JOHN SHEDDEN

THE CROWOOD PRESS

First published in 1986 by
THE CROWOOD PRESS
Crowood House, Ramsbury
Marlborough, Wiltshire SN8 2HE

Paperback edition 1987
Reprinted 1989

British Library Cataloguing in Publication Data

Shedden, John
Skiing : developing your skill
1. Skis and skiing
I. Title
796.93 GV854

ISBN 0 946284 42 3 (HB)
1 85223 094 0 (PB)

Acknowledgements

I would like to thank Alan Hughes in association with whom I wrote Chapters 2 and 4, and Colin Whiteside on whose thinking these chapters draw. Chapter 6 is modelled on the work that Stan Palmer has done for the National Junior Squads. These three are more than skiing colleagues and personal friends, they are men who have given a significant part of their lives to improving not only the skiing but the understanding and attitudes of others in the ski world and we are all the richer for their work. My thanks also to Europa Sport and Kent Shuss for the use of ski equipment.

Photographs by LSI Computers (Fig 63), Nic Fellows (Figs 91, 92 and 93) and Salamon (Figs 31, 33, 34, 35, 86, 103); all others by author.

Series Adviser David Bunker, Lecturer, University of Loughborough

Typeset by Lee Educational
Printed in Great Britain by Redwood Burn Ltd, Trowbridge

Contents

John Shedden is the English Ski Council's Director of Coaching. During his extensive career he has been involved with a wide range of skiers and ski instructors both in Britain and overseas. He was appointed Director of Coaching for the National Ski Federation of Great Britain in 1975, and designed and developed their coaching scheme. Since his appointment to his current post in 1979, he has concentrated on improving the education of skiers and instructors in this country. His books include *Ski Teaching*, *Learning to Ski* and *Skilful Skiing*.

It was many years ago that I first met John Shedden, when we were both enthusiastic newcomers to ski teaching. In the time since then, John has contributed many refreshing ideas about teaching and has helped countless people, from recreational skiers to international competitors, to learn and to improve. His complete dedication to the sport of skiing and his questioning of its accepted beliefs have made all of John's writings on ski technique essential and thought-provoking reading – not just for pupils, but also for ski teachers, since we too are still learning.

Alasdair Ross

Coaching – as opposed to ski instruction – is still very scarce in Britain. John, who invented ski coaching as far as English skiers are concerned, has guided my long-term growth as a ski racer. His knowledge and ability have helped me develop technically, physically and mentally.

Books cannot substitute for a personal coach but I am sure that John's approach to learning to ski, expressed in this book, will help every skier who reads it.

Sarah Lewis *British Alpine Team Member*
All England and British Slalom Champion

Introduction

'Don't look down at your skis!' Familiar advice to anyone who has taken formal lessons in a ski school. My advice to beginners in the same circumstances would probably be 'look at your skis, now watch where you are going'. This sort of comment will be evident throughout the book. It is not, as it may appear at first sight, contradictory advice. This specific example will be explained in Chapter 4, but in more general terms my aim is to give *positive*, rather than the all too common negative, advice, and furthermore to amplify and explain what your ski instructor or coach means when giving ski lessons. When you are having lessons as a beginner or taking more advanced coaching your instructor or coach should tell you *what to do* rather than why. This saves valuable time as too much explanation can detract from the real purpose of a lesson or coaching session – *practice*. Only through practice will you learn and improve.

In these pages I shall explain some of the reasons for practising as you should in order to get the most out of your time spent skiing downhill. My intention is to give you a clear and simple idea of what learning to ski is all about and to enable

Fig 1 'Don't look down at your skis!'

Fig 2 The author skiing with Britain's best technical lady skier, Sarah Lewis, on an exhilarating early morning 'powder run'.

you to understand the structure of the sport so that you may take responsibility for your own progress and gain as much enjoyment from your skiing as I have from mine.

There are only three major points to bear in mind for the development of successful skiing.

1. *Seek advice* from well-qualified instructors and experienced coaches.
2. Read, discuss, ask questions and think about your skiing before and after but never during your skiing.
3. When you are moving on skis *feel* what you are doing and what is happening to you.

It is the *feelings* of skiing which are not only the key to progress but the ultimate source of enjoyment and exhilaration which skiing gives.

This book will give you hints and advice and I hope it will also help you to understand what you should be doing and what is happening to you when you ski, but this alone is not enough. The rest and the best part is up to you. *Go skiing*! *Feel* the excitement of movement powered by gravity and the exhilaration won by mastering control of your self and your skis as you slide through the crystal-clear air, in communion with nature in all her winter beauty – safe in a hostile environment – seeking harmony with the mountain.

1 Skiing with Skill

As a fifteen year old I had never seen a mountain. On 27 December 1958 I travelled with a school party, in heavy rain or fog every yard of the journey, to Wengen in the Bernese Oberland. The fine drizzle changed to snow when we arrived the following evening, and it continued snowing for three more days. In the small dormitories of the Hotel Waldegg we washed in a basin with freezing water from an ornate and flowered jug. On the morning of New Year's Day I was the first to rise. I reached past the bowl and jug to open the windows and retrieve my soap from the window-ledge outside. The windows were covered in frozen conden-

Fig 3 'My very first view of a mountain.' The immense grandeur of the Jungfrau at dawn filled me with a respect and awe which has never diminished.

Fig 4 To think of ski technique alone is to miss the whole point of skiing.

sation. Jack Frost's curtains obscured the outside world and kept me quite unprepared for my first visual encounter with a mountain. The snow had stopped in the night and the clear air was biting cold as I opened the window. At first I could not take in the immense grandeur of the view before me. The first rays of the early morning sun were just catching the summit ridge of the Jungfrau. The vertical distance from the valley floor to peak must be over 10,000 feet and the gasps of surprise and wonder from my room-mates told me that they were as surprised and as impressed as I was. Impressed is too simple, too inadequate a word to really express the true awe that I felt in those moments. It was simply 'love at first sight' and my respect, love and enjoyment of the mountains has never diminished.

Being on mountains, moving among them and feeling their ever-changing moods is a major part of the thrill and excitement of skiing. Getting to know them, learning how they behave (for they are very much 'alive') and learning how to live in harmony with them is a very important part of skiing skill. To think of ski techniques alone is to miss the point of it all. Yet without technical proficiency you will be a danger to yourself and others in what is both a most beautiful and yet potentially very hostile world. Developing your skill as a skier is learning new techniques, but also applying them to the hillside so that you move comfortably with and never in opposition to the mountains.

It was on this first day that I began to

understand the difference between technique for its own sake and skilful application of techniques in the terrain. I learned also that there were good instructors and poor ones. My attitude to ski instructors was forged that day, when I realised that Hans, our Swiss instructor, was not teaching us to ski he was simply working his way through his instructor's manual. We had been taught to schuss, to plough and to sidestep and, having practised on our own every afternoon, we were thrilled with our ability to mix these up and ski down a field back to our hotel by the evening of the third day. We had learned how to steer our ploughs and link them with a skid by drawing the inner ski towards the outer. When we showed Hans our newly developed skill, far from being impressed and much to our dismay and disappointment, he expressed anger at our efforts and told us to stop them at once. It may have been that we were skiing dangerously or with poor technical elements, but that was not why Hans told us to stop. He said simply, 'You are not supposed to learn that until next week'. We were returning to England in three days' time and would not be there 'next week' to have another go at what we felt we could do already. We were all demoralised and took scant notice of Hans from then on. It is significant to me that only three of us ever went skiing again and I am sure Hans' attitude helped to put all the others in my class off skiing for ever.

I hope you will never meet an instructor like Hans but you may find yourself following instructions you do not understand or being asked to do exercises or activities which seem pointless or even contradictory to activities you have learned previously. If your instructor is qualified persevere but never be afraid to ask why you are doing something if you do not understand. To aid your understanding, the rest of this book should help to put your activities in perspective.

SKILL DEFINED

You may think it odd that I should feel the need to try to define skill; it is, however, a relatively new concept in ski instruction. For far too long traditional National Ski Schools, selling ski lessons to holidaymakers, have concentrated on ski techniques and failed to consider their application to either the individual skiers learning them or the terrain on which they are being learned and used. The desire to teach uniform methods in all ski schools by all ski instructors of that nation has often meant that dogma has emerged which is removed from the *needs* of individual pupils and orientated towards the needs of the ski school administration. To those of us who ski for fun it is a sport, a leisure activity, but in Austria it is a major industry and many of the ski instructor associations which attempt to emulate the Austrians fail to grasp this point and may thus provide a less than complete service for their pupils. Uniform technique, although an attractive idea, can never give the complete satisfaction of versatile and individual skill.

Skill is the ability that an individual skier has when he is able to set realistic goals or tasks and achieve them effectively, consistently, with efficient movements and under a wide range of environmental conditions. A skilful skier is versatile and adaptable and far from having perfect technique habits will probably never make exactly the same movements twice in succession.

To develop skill you must therefore learn

as wide a variety of techniques as you can master. You must learn to adapt them to all sorts of terrain and snow conditions. You must learn to judge what you can and cannot achieve on any single occasion and monitor what you are doing to ensure that you remain safe and in control all the time, changing your mind if necessary about what you can achieve and how you might achieve it.

Skill is evidenced in actions not words. A skilful performance is a result of learning but will be determined on any single occasion by the interplay of your judgement, objectives, emotions, fitness and your technical competence and versatility. Judgements are possible as a direct consequence of your perceptual processes, which enable you to give meaning to your own movements and the environment you are in.

The extent of your skill will be determined by the quality and breadth of your perception, your emotional state and general emotional disposition and the quality, variety and appropriateness of the techniques which you select in order to achieve a specific goal. Development of one of these factors will have a profound effect on the other two and so change the level of your skill. All three will be affected by your state of fitness and so growth in your skill requires improvement in all three areas together with concurrent improvement in your fitness.

Fig 5 Nigel Smith, British Team Member and principally a downhill racer, demonstrates his versatility with effective, efficient slalom technique in soft summer snow on the Tignes glacier.

Establishing Goals

To achieve the most satisfaction from your learning you should try to establish both short-term objectives and long-term aims. You can measure your skill by the achievement of these objectives and the manner of your achievement.

Two major aims of most skiers are either good style, elegance and aesthetic satisfaction or competition and racing success. These aims are not mutually exclusive as what works for the racer at extremes of control is usually functionally sound and therefore stylish and elegant if performed under more controlled and less demanding conditions.

Style and Elegance

In order to ski with good style and glide apparently effortlessly over the slopes you will need considerable skill. You will need to judge your terrain carefully, control your speed and ski within the limits of your ability.

'Posing' or trying to look good for its own sake will normally produce stilted and awkward movements and positions. True elegance and style comes from functionally sound movements executed with impeccable judgement, superb anticipation and split-second timing – all the ingredients that are required in the skill of the competitive skier.

Fig 6 'What works for the racer is functionally sound', as Sarah Lewis shows when she tackles soft powder snow – a complete contrast from the normally hard and icy piste of the slalom race course.

Fig 7 Personal excellence is often an expression of personality.

These two aims are perhaps more an expression of personality and can be reached on similar routes by skiers with different attitudes to their skiing.

Personal Excellence
(Figs 7 & 8)

Appreciated subjectively by the quality of movement sensations and recognised objectively by the variety of terrain in which you can ski or the level of competition at which you succeed, personal excellence is only achieved by developing your strong points, working on and improving your weaknesses and continually changing what you are doing.

Work from one objective to another. Set yourself small and specific tasks every time you ski, and incorporate into all your activities on skis the following objectives which will lead you towards your own long-term aims.

Objective 1 – Control
(Figs 9 to 11)

When you first put on boots and skis they will feel so awkward and heavy that you will wonder how anyone could ever be elegant or athletic wearing such things. Your first objective therefore is to move around on a level and safe area so that you can learn how to control your equipment.

Control of your equipment and yourself are inextricably linked because you can only control your skis by moving your own muscles. *Inertia* and *entropy* are the interesting factors here, because left to their own devices your skis and boots will do absolutely nothing and will try to persuade your legs and feet to do the same. If you find yourself on a hill then of course they will tend to try to get to the bottom as quickly and directly as possible and take you with them. You must not let them!

Work your legs and feet so that you *dominate* your equipment and can exercise refined control over it. This is your first objective and also your main continuing objective. Your task changes with changes in the terrain: when you move onto a slope, onto a steeper slope, down a slope, down a longer slope with changes in gradient or surface textures and when you want to slow down, stop or change direction.

Remember your objective in all these tasks is to control your equipment and to control yourself. Whenever you feel you are inhibited by your boots or being carried passively by your skis, act positively and make decisive movements which will enable you to dominate your equipment. To do this effectively adopt the following *tactics*:

1. Use your *judgement* to determine the outcome of your movements. What effect – precisely – will they have?
2. Move positively but sensitively: *feel* what is happening to you. Use your vision, hearing and touch to 'tell you' if your initial judgements were sound and then correct if it is necessary. The better your initial judgement, the smaller and easier the corrections will be.
3. When you have finished, assess your actions.

Fig 8 Personal excellence can be realised in many forms of skiing from the freedom for self-expression in off piste skiing to the choice of steps on the ascending ladder of competition.

Fig 9 'Will I ever get the hang of this?'

Fig 10 OBJECTIVE 1. Dominate your equipment so that you can move athletically as easily with skis on as you can without them.

Fig 11 There is always a tendency for big and seemingly awkward ski boots to carry you along where they want to take you. Your first and continuing objective is to work your legs and especially your ankles to make your equipment work for you.

It does not matter if your initial judgements were not accurate or your movements did not achieve what you intended. If you follow the three tactics your rate of learning will increase rapidly and you will soon be exercising good control over your skis.

Objective 2 – Versatility *(Fig 12)*

Whether your aim is style and elegance or success in competition it is worth remembering that 'no two turns are ever the same'. As you learn and develop as a skier it is important to avoid developing habits of movement or posture that you do not monitor in action. Remember the twins – inertia and entropy? Given half a chance our bodies will do as little as possible and use simple habits if the conditions seem right.

Of course, you must develop *automatic responses* in your techniques, but always look at the terrain very carefully and follow the three tactics described above. Be alert to changes in the terrain and surface texture and modify your movements accordingly. Thus as your versatility improves you must develop adaptability of thought as well as technique. Practise techniques until they are automatic, but never mistake technical competence for skill.

In your search for excellence you will need to recognise increasingly subtle changes in the surface terrain and textures, to predict accurately the effects they will have on you and the effects you can achieve in them. You will need to control the fundamental actions of your skis, the edging, turning and pressuring of them, from extremes of body shapes and under many differences in terrain and snow

Fig 12 OBJECTIVE 2. When you can steer as your legs bend, learn also to steer as your legs extend. Develop a wide repertoire of techniques – be versatile.

conditions. When you can steer a ski as your leg is bending you must also be able to steer it when your leg is extending, if you are to cope successfully with all the varieties of terrain you will find on an open mountainside.

Your second main and continuing objective will be to develop a wide repertoire of techniques – to learn how to perform the essential elements of all techniques in a wide variety of ways. This will increase the choices you have to make in any single condition, but it will also increase the choices you can make about where, when and how you ski over the whole length and height of the mountains.

Competition

In its simplest form this is usually thought of as racing. Competition is, however, really testing yourself against outside 'opposition' or standards. In the case of the slalom racer the opposition is the course, the stop-watch and the ability of the other racers; such competition, demanding as it is, can be great fun if the opposition factors are not too severe. Just as satisfying, however, is the competition of putting your own ability now against your ability yesterday by measuring it in Personal Performance Factor Award Schemes.

Fig 13 Despite its extensive jargon skiing is really very simple and is best appreciated in the high mountains, in the company of friends with whom you can share the experience.

Skiing with Skill

Despite its extensive jargon and seemingly complex dynamics, skiing is really very simple: 'You just point your feet where you want to go and stay (sort of) above them whilst you make them go there'. To achieve this you must keep returning to your two main objectives whilst learning. Make your body and thus your equipment do what you intend it to do, and do it sensitively and efficiently, in harmony with the mountainside. Achievement of these two objectives is the source of most of your satisfaction and exhilaration in skiing. The remaining pleasure and joy comes from appreciation of the mountains and nature at the limits of our biosphere, and from the company of friends with whom you can share these experiences.

2 Acquiring Skill

As Director of Coaching for the National Coaching Scheme I work from a simple philosophy: that is, *you have ability*. The instructional and coaching methods of the whole National Coaching Scheme from the Club Instructors and Artificial Slope Ski Instructors (ASSI) to the Staff Coaches are based on this philosophy. As coaches we start from the assumption that the pupil – expert or beginner – already has ability. That is to say that if you want to learn how to ski or how to ski better we have to start from where you are now. We set you an easy task and then observe you closely, assessing your strengths and weaknesses and the extent of your skill.

If skill is the ability to do (effectively, efficiently and consistently) what you *intend* to do, then our job as coaches and instructors is to enable your body to learn 'to do as it is told' by you and then to increase the difficulty and variety of the tasks that you give yourself – and at which you still succeed. We do this within a framework, a *syllabus*. This syllabus has a developmental pattern and is designed to enable you to progress along a continuum – developing your skill steadily from that of a non-skier to that of an advanced recreational skier. We begin our syllabus on dry or artificial ski slopes.

Dry Ski Slopes *(Figs 14 & 15)*

These were first constructed in the early 1960s and very soon provided the ideal medium for beginners to learn on. More than seventy-five per cent of our National Squads did their early training on dry ski slopes and continue to do basic training on them today. These slopes are called dry slopes because they are made from (in the main) PVC rather than snow. On the other hand they run more easily and give more skiing pleasure when they are wet, either from rain or from sprinklers such as those installed at the Gloucester and Silksworth slopes. Whilst the slopes are artificial the skiing done on them is very real, but not, of course, comprehensive or complete. It can therefore be argued that you cannot learn to ski completely on a dry slope. The range of surface textures, gradients and terrain forms will always be limited. Indeed skiing is truly of the mountains and we use dry slopes to learn part of the whole sport and to eliminate some of the undesirable variables (extreme snow or ice conditions) and thus make learning easier for beginners.

ASSI Syllabus

This syllabus is simple and direct. I will indicate the stages which we consider important and explain the thinking behind the activities which you may be asked to do by your instructor when you take ski lessons. In describing it I may give the impression that a particular form of demonstration (by the instructor) or action (by the learner) is especially important. Where this is done you should not infer that I am advocating a uniform technique or an ASSI way of doing a manoeuvre. As you have already seen versatility and

Fig 14 More than seventy-five per cent of our National Squads learned on dry ski slopes.

Fig 15 Nic Fellows, winner of the 1985 Grand Prix, learned on a dry ski slope.

adaptability are the corner-stones of skill development. The reason for stressing a particular technical element or movement pattern is to encourage technically sound and safe movements which work not only now – on 'this' slope – but which will lend themselves most easily to adaptation on other terrain and surfaces, and which will continue to be effective, and in some cases be more effective, at higher speeds on steeper slopes and on the snow.

We want not only to teach you to solve today's skiing tasks, but more importantly to prepare you to learn *for* and *in* the future, wherever that further learning may take place. In this respect the advice and explanations which follow will apply equally as well if you take lessons in a mountain ski resort or ski school.

The Beginnings (*Fig 16*)

You will start on level terrain and spend up to twenty or thirty minutes walking, turning, running and even perhaps skating on level terrain. You will attempt to manoeuvre in all directions within the pattern shown in *Fig 16*. You may also be encouraged to play relay races or other games at this time. The reason for this is to get used to the equipment. When you arrived at the ski centre you could walk, run, turn and generally move in an athletic manner – now you must accept that your body 'knows' how to do these things but it is inhibited by your equipment. Your boots seem stiff and heavy and your 'feet' are very long and awkward.

Remember the first objective. You are in

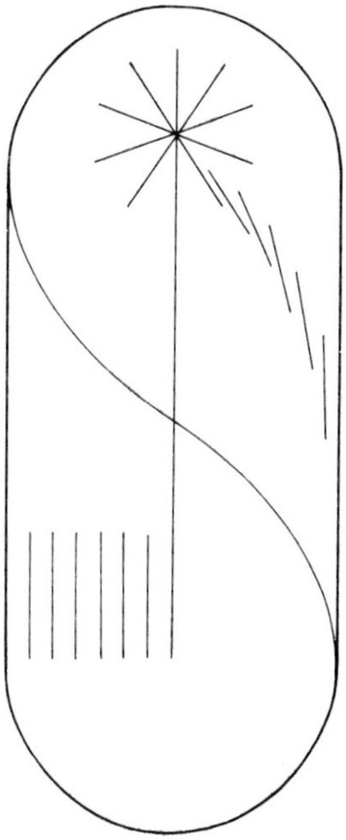

Fig 16 Learn to control your equipment and move around athletically on the pathways indicated above.

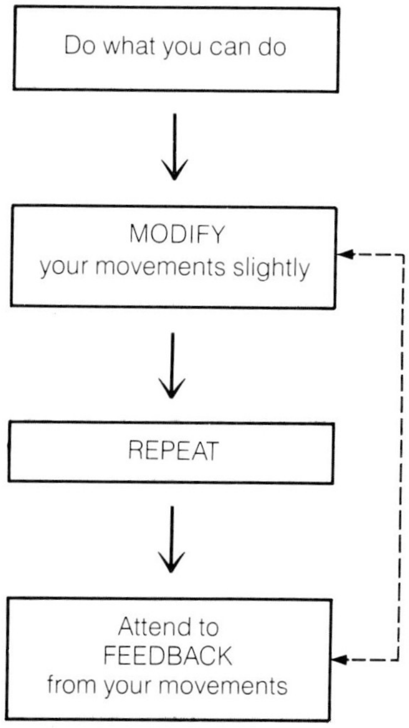

Fig 17 The learning method.

charge – dominate your equipment. Make sure your ankles flex and extend. Slide your skis along the surface and steer them parallel. As a non-skier you will tend to stand normally with your feet slightly splayed and perhaps to run in this manner too. To be a good skier you must modify your stance and your athletic movements so that your feet and skis slide and remain parallel – unless you intend them to be otherwise. This illustrates the approach that we adopt in our coaching and which I will encourage you to accept as your method of making progress.

The Learning Method *(Fig 17)*

1. Begin by doing what you *can* do.
2. *Modify* your movements slightly.
3. Learn by *repeating* these modified movements which you can now do.
4. Appropriate *feedback* will encourage you, increase your accuracy and improve your success rate. So watch, listen and feel what you are doing; assess but do not judge yourself.

The learning method is therefore very simple. I do not want you ever to attempt a new manoeuvre – a manoeuvre that you cannot yet do. I want you only to *modify* what you can do until you are doing something else. Learning and development are continuous processes. They are not achieved by trying to jump to the next step or next technique and failing. Progress is a process of successful modification of what you can already do. I will develop this

Fig 18 As a skier you learn how to move in an environment that is fundamentally different from that of non-skiers.

Fig 19 Nordic or cross-country skiing is an ideal way of bridging the world of non-skiers and the world of skiers (alpine). The light equipment and level terrain will enable you to move athletically on a slippery, featureless world before making the next move onto the tilted world where gravity will generate your motion.

theme in later chapters, but for now I will return to the syllabus – the framework of your progress and learning and the principles which underlie its structure

Flow and Resist (Figs 18 to 20)

As a skier you have to move in an environment that is fundamentally different from that of non-skiers. It smells, sounds, feels and looks different. Most of your problems as a beginner stem from these differences. It will take time to get used to them, to adjust your understanding of 'how things work'. Initially your perceptions will be faulty, and you need to become familiar with your new surroundings before you will be able to move as athletically in them as you could in the world of non-skiers.

Non-skiers live in a world that is relatively level and smooth; it is sticky (shoes grip at every step) and is marked with corners, straight lines and edges. Skiers live in a tilted world with great undulations; it is very slippery and is relatively featureless. Non-skiers use their muscles to generate movement and propel them; skiers are powered by gravity and use their muscles for control and steering.

In mechanical or technical terms the movements of skiing – the ski techniques – are quite simple. Your difficulties as a beginner arise from your perceptions of yourself and this new environment.

Because of these problems of orientation and the inhibiting nature of your equipment, you will tend to stand still or move only slowly and defensively. When you descend your first gentle slope you will find that you can slide downhill by doing very little and by keeping your body quite still. You will be able to get away with using a *static balance* mode. At higher speeds and when you are more able to read the terrain this static balance mode will not work. You must therefore spend most of your time as a beginner on the nursery slopes, developing a dynamic approach to balancing. You must avoid 'static' motion (*see* Chapter 3) and reorientate yourself in your new environment.

All the activities that you do as a beginner will enable you to achieve this and develop your athletic ability on skis, by regaining much of the athletic ability that you already had before you put on skis and boots.

When you move onto the slope you begin to recognise the two central characters of skiing, the two ingredients with which you must come to terms in order to develop your ability as a skier: *flow* and *resist*. Flow is the tendency to go downhill. This is strongest when you are on a steep, smooth hill or when you are moving

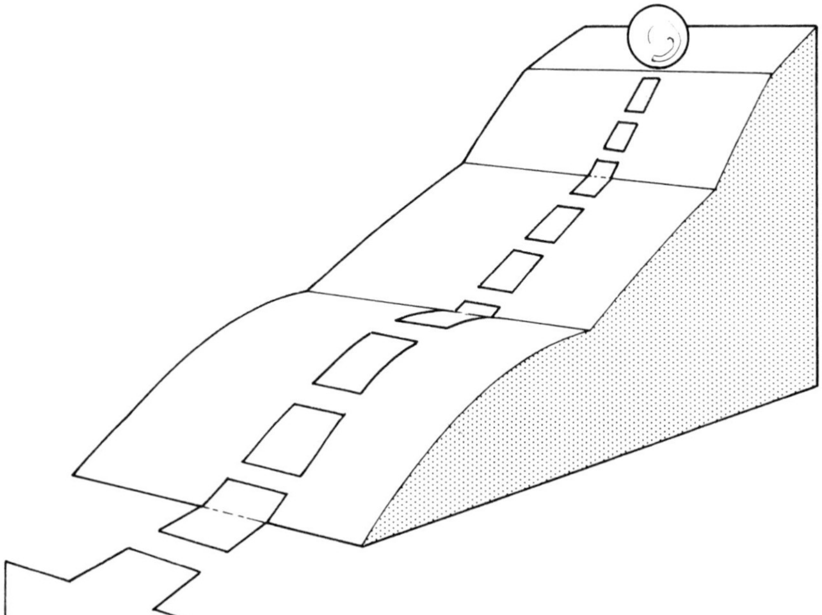

Fig 20 The fall line. The tendency to flow is strongest on steep slopes or when you are moving quickly. Recognition of your fall line from wherever you are on the hillside is the first task you must solve when you move onto a slope to ski.

quickly, and weakest on shallow or level terrain. From any single point on a hillside consider the path of a rolling ball or the direction that flowing water will take. The pathway – this 'line' which follows the contours of the hillside – is called, in the language of the Alps, the fall line. The fall line is the source of our motive power on skis. Point your skis down it and you will flow downhill.

Fig 21 As an expert skier you will be able to resist but also to flow – emotionally as well as physically – down all sorts of gradients and at all sorts of speeds.

Learning to Flow *(Fig 21)*

Much of your first lesson will be spent sidestepping, with your skis at right angles to your flow line in order that you can gain sufficient height up the slope to enjoy your first free runs powered only by gravity.

By edging your skis, they grip for you and enable you to push or even thrust sideways. By edging with your skis across the slope, you resist the tendency to flow.

By turning and edging your skis across your flow line you will prevent your skis from sliding, and if later when you are in motion you do the same, you will offer resistance to your flow. You will use this resistance to bring your flow under control. You will find *resisting* a perfectly normal thing to do – all our normal movements off skis occur because we resist with our feet. Think of trying to run about on sheet ice with smooth leather-soled shoes and you will see what I mean. Resisting is easy so you must learn to flow with equal ease.

During your lessons you will make repeated descents down the flow line. This is sometimes called *schussing* or straight running. You should schuss long and often – always into a safe run-out area so that you do not have to concern yourself with stopping – and so concentrate on developing sensitive *dynamic balance*. There are many techniques which you can use when flowing, but the vital point about flow is that you enjoy it. Practise flowing until you are very confident and can allow yourself to flow emotionally as well as physically downhill. To become an expert skier you will need to let yourself flow down all sorts of gradients and terrain at all sorts of speeds. The ultimate in flowing, the world speed record on skis, is over 120 miles per hour – achieved in a simple schuss by flowing with minimum resistance down a very steep and smooth slope.

However, you will only allow yourself to flow with confidence if you know you can in some way control yourself and your flow. If the flow line is like the accelerator pedal in a car, knowing how to use the brakes and steering gives you confidence and presence of mind to drive your car well, even if you do not use the brakes all that often. Thus you can only allow yourself to flow happily and safely if you know how to resist. In the early lessons you can concentrate on flow without having to know how to resist (whilst in motion) because the run-out area will bring you to a safe halt. In later lessons you will learn how to resist whilst you are flowing.

The very *essence* of skilful skiing is balancing your flow and resistance in harmony with the terrain.

The ideal method for developing this balance between flow and resist is to use the funnel.

The Funnel *(Figs 22 & 23)*

The funnel is both a spatial and temporal concept which, if you ski within it, will enable you to develop your skill and progress along a continuum from basic schussing through continuously varying forms of techniques to advanced parallel skiing, making linked turns staying close to the flow line but in perfectly balanced control of self and skis.

The shape of the funnel at its beginning and end is only a metre or so wide, and it opens in the middle area to perhaps twenty or thirty metres wide. You will ski within its shape, but you will use as much of its width as you can without going outside the shape. The length of the funnel is between three hundred and six hundred

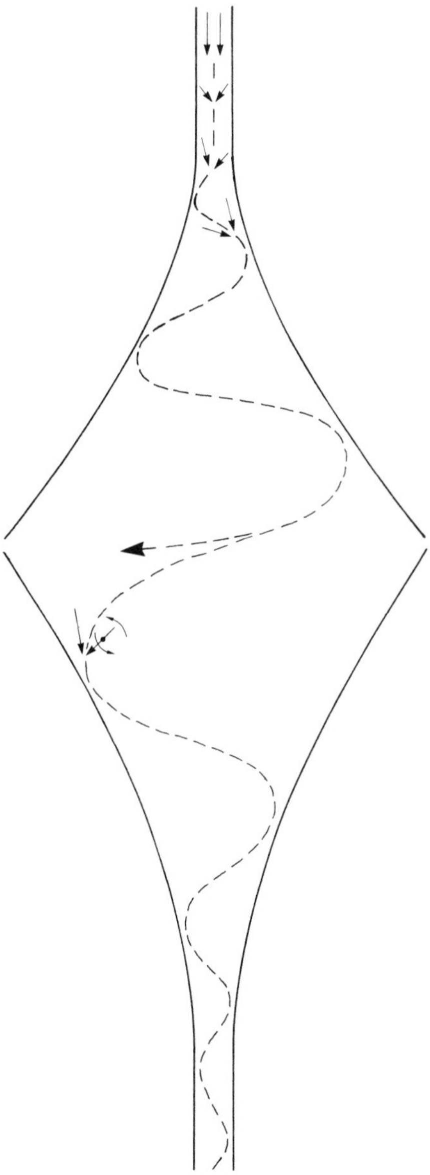

Fig 22 *The funnel. This is your target. As you modify your movements and develop skiing techniques apply them – very accurately – to the funnel. Use your technical ability to ski to the exact edge of the funnel. Solving this task will cause and allow small modifications to your movements – to what you can already do – and so your ability to direct your flow will develop skilfully.*

metres depending upon the variations in terrain and gradient. Its length will also be between twelve hours and five or six weeks, depending upon your rate of progress and learning.

At the beginning of this chapter I said that you will progress by modifying what you can already do. You will change the task from time to time and modify your movements (your technique) in order to solve the new task. The funnel tells you what the tasks are. The funnel helps you to modify your technique to achieve differing forms of control by changing the relationship between flow and resist. Your instructor will guide you down the funnel and show you how to modify what you are doing – dependent upon where you are in the funnel – in order to prepare you to ski the next part of the funnel.

Rhythm and Patterns

During your descent of the funnel your emotional states will change. Your perception will develop and you will become comfortably orientated on the hillside. Your state of motion will change and this will influence your posture and techniques, but in order to achieve the maximum benefit from skiing the funnel you must change the nature of your movements.

When you enter the funnel you will make, for the most part, single, simple movements. As you descend the funnel you will learn to link movements together. In the lower part of the funnel you will develop the optimum balance between flowing freely and feeling a sense of mastery and control over your descent when you add *rhythm* to *patterns* of movements which you perform within the shape of the funnel, in harmony with the undulations of the terrain.

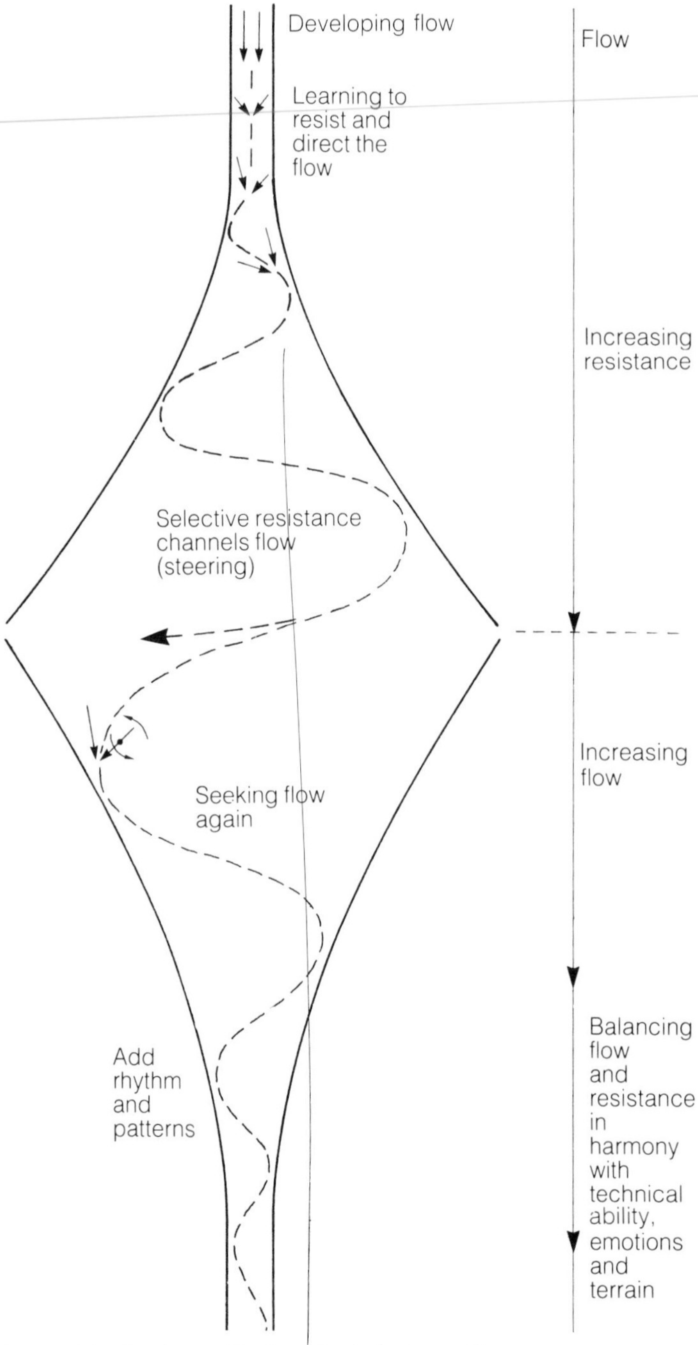

Fig 23 By using the target, i.e. the shape of the funnel, to help you modify your movements — continuously — you will learn to balance your ability to resist with your tendency to flow. You will develop your technical competence into skill.

3 Movements and Motion

In everyday conversation the words motion and movement normally have the same meaning. It will be valuable for your development as a skier if you distinguish between them in the manner described in this chapter. *Skiing is movements in motion.* Traditionally, ski instructors teach body movements – the combinations of these movements are called ski techniques. For example, the technique of snowploughing is achieved by the movements of rotation and abduction of the legs, usually with flexion (bending) of the ankles, knees and hips. The movements of snowploughing are usually done at slow speeds or at slow motion.

In *Skilful Skiing* (1982), I showed how the *motion* of the skier will affect his movements, and considered Newton's Laws of Motion to explain how and why. For example, skidding can only occur when the skier is travelling – when he has motion. Skidding occurs when one or both skis are turned at an angle to the direction of motion of the skier – across his line of momentum. Side-slipping, on the other hand, can occur when the skier is initially stationary – when he has no motion. By releasing the 'grip' of the skis across the flow line, achieved with movements of the body, the initially stationary skier slips – he begins to move, he acquires motion. In this chapter I shall consider the relationship of your movements to your motion.

Because the traditional approach to ski instruction has usually been to consider only techniques, only movements of the body, and to virtually ignore their relationships to the terrain and the motion of the skier, I was especially impressed with the courage as well as the clarity of expression from the Canadian presentation at the Interski Congress in Sexton, Italy, in 1983. With their demonstrations they gave the following specific working definitions to these words:

Motion relates to the passage or path of the skier's centre of mass as he travels down the slope.

Movement is the displacement of body segments (arms, calves, thighs etc) relative to each other.

Looking at skiing from this point of view enables us to see that our movements and our motion are caused and influenced by different sources of force. Movements are caused by muscles; motion is caused by gravity. In addition, however, friction, snow resistance and inertia or momentum influence our movements and motion.

States of Motion *(Fig 24)*

In the world of non-skiers we generate motion and movements by our body. Such motion and movements are called athletic. In skiing you can create motion in the same way on level ground, but as the slopes become steeper gravity increasingly influences your motion. You will now use your muscles to influence your motion (caused by gravity) by adding to it – pushing, skating etc – or by directing and steering it through *resisting*.

When you wish to influence your motion significantly then you should move in an athletic manner. You will feel yourself to be athletic. On the other hand, once you have begun to slide or flow downhill you may, on smooth slopes, be able to remain quite still without losing balance. This stillness of your body, this quietness of movement, may continue as you slide in motion because as long as the slope is smooth and regular you will not need to move in order to adjust your balance. In this form of motion your movements or lack of them could be termed *static*.

You can see, therefore, that the motion of the body is influenced by its movements and progress between static and athletic. These states of movement in motion relate also to the *balance mode* that your body is using. As you move from static into athletic movements so you must change your balance from static to dynamic.

As the slope becomes steeper and your speed increases, your own momentum influences your motion in addition to gravity. At this point you will feel that you are being carried along by your own motion, and your movements may have relatively little effect on your motion. This is called *ballistic motion*. In ballistic motion the possibility of influencing that motion by your movements or techniques still exists, but the influences will not cause immediate change. You must therefore think, look and plan well ahead and remain calm emotionally.

It is probable that as a beginner you felt ballistic when you were making your first descents. You soon learned, however, that with confidence and good control of yourself and your equipment you were able to become athletic and so step, jump, steer and so on satisfactorily. This is always possible if you remember your first objective: dominate your equipment, be in charge of your own movements.

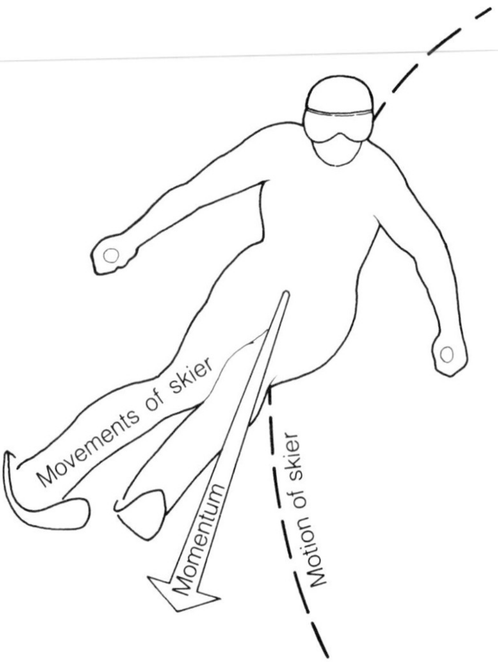

Fig 24 Movements in motion.

Your state of motion at any time will, therefore, be a consequence of your emotional state, your perceptions and intentions and your movements or techniques. All these factors will be influenced by your balance mode – the way in which you attempt to stay, roughly, above your feet. It is useful to relate your developing states of motion as a skier to the balance modes which will be necessary to achieve them.

Dynamic Balance

In Chapter 2 I said that skiing, despite all the jargon and technical mystique, is really very simple. 'You just point your feet where

Fig 25 As you move into athletic movements so you must adopt anticipatory, dynamic balance.

you want to go and stay (sort of) above them whilst you make them go there.' Pointing your feet where you want to go and making them go there are what ski techniques – our movements – are all about. On the other hand, staying above the feet is what balancing is all about and this is also movement.

We balance by responding to forces which would otherwise upset us, but as our motion increases and we become athletic or ballistic we must not only respond but also act positively in advance by anticipating the influences of the terrain ahead on our movements and motion and the action we intend to take. Anticipation is a mental process, it involves your perception and your intentions. It can be seen in the way you prepare to balance in motion. Such *anticipatory balance* is another way of thinking of dynamic balance.

As a beginner you found your boots and skis heavy and awkward; they inhibited your movements and probably influenced you to use static balance or a responsive balance mode. In your first downhill runs you probably felt ballistic – even at two or three miles per hour. These feelings are quite normal because your body balances in two entirely different modes depending upon its perceived states of motion. When you perceive yourself to be still – neither moving nor in motion – your body adopts a responsive or static balance mode. When you are athletic or in a comfortable and confident ballistic state of motion you will use the anticipatory or dynamic balancing mode. If, however, you are defensive when you feel yourself to be ballistic you may adopt some aspects of the static balance mode; this would be undesirable as you will lose the facility to anticipate successfully. For example, if you are ballistic you can only slow down; therefore you will tend to lean backwards in order to absorb the expected deceleration when it happens. Such 'self defence' is not always advisable and often creates a vicious circle. It will be useful to compare the two balance modes so that you can actively change from one to the other.

Dynamic balance differs from static balance in six major ways.

1. *Eyes.* In the static mode these may be open or closed, and the head may be tilted to one side. In the dynamic mode the eye line must be horizontal, the eyes must be alert and looking closely at the terrain ahead.
2. *Joints.* In the static mode the legs will be straight or almost straight and the body is 'tall' and upright; while in the dynamic the ankles, knees and hips flex and the body lowers.
3. *Weight.* In the static mode this is carried through the heels and the outside edges of the feet. In the dynamic mode the weight is supported by the whole of the feet and the front inside edges are used for propulsion and control of movements.
4. *Centre of mass.* This will be above the feet in the static mode; while in the dynamic mode it will not be above the feet, but as the legs incline it will move inwards as you turn.
5. *Arms.* In the static mode the arms will hang from the shoulders and lie close to the body; while in the dynamic they will become alert and move out and forwards – as if holding a hoop.
6. *Pelvis.* In the static mode the pelvis tends to tilt downwards, whereas in the dynamic it must tilt upwards.

Style

When you join a ski class you may find that your instructor places a lot of emphasis on his style. If so it is vital for your progress as a skier that his style is based upon sound posture and good dynamic balance. Style for its own sake which inhibits, in any way, good dynamic balance will prevent the development of skilful skiing. The quality of your skiing will depend upon your ability to harmonise your movements in motion – to enhance your dynamic balance. Sadly, this is often neglected in formal ski instruction within ski schools and so you should give considerable attention yourself to improving the quality of your dynamic (anticipatory) balance by attending to the following six factors which will influence it most of all.

Eyes (Fig 26)

Your eye line should be horizontal. Your eyes are vital for judging the terrain ahead of you. Keep your head as quiet as possible and so enable your eyes to see clearly within a steady frame of reference. The

Fig 26 Despite considerable changes of movements and motion, dynamic balance is enhanced by keeping the eye line horizontal.

balance mechanisms in your inner ear will also function most effectively if your head is quiet and your eye line horizontal.

Flexion (Fig 27)

In order to cope both physically and emotionally with speed your body will normally crouch or flex. This is very appropriate in skiing and you should do it consciously. Flex at your ankles, knees and hips simultaneously and always incline your trunk (upper body) at least as much as you incline your shins. When you begin to flex, move your shoulders down and forwards. As you learn to cope with increasing speed progressively straighten up; in this way you will keep 'flex' in reserve to enable you to move into higher speeds.

Weight (Figs 28 & 29)

Your feet are complex structures, each having twenty-six different small bones. The construction of your feet allows them to fulfil two functions; they can act as a support or as propulsive levers. Because the bones at the back of your feet are bigger than those at the front, the heels are most suitable to bear your weight. Also because your feet are arched – both longitudinally and medially – your weight is carried to the outer edges of your feet. It is therefore normal to stand on your heels and outer edges if all you are doing is supporting your weight. On the other hand, in order to act as propulsive levers your feet must be 'tensioned' and pivot about the balls of the feet. This tensioning is achieved by flexing your ankles. This

Fig 27 We cope with speed by flexing. Whenever you learn new movements or apply learned ones at higher speeds, always crouch slightly, bending ankles as well as hips. Always incline your trunk as much as your shins.

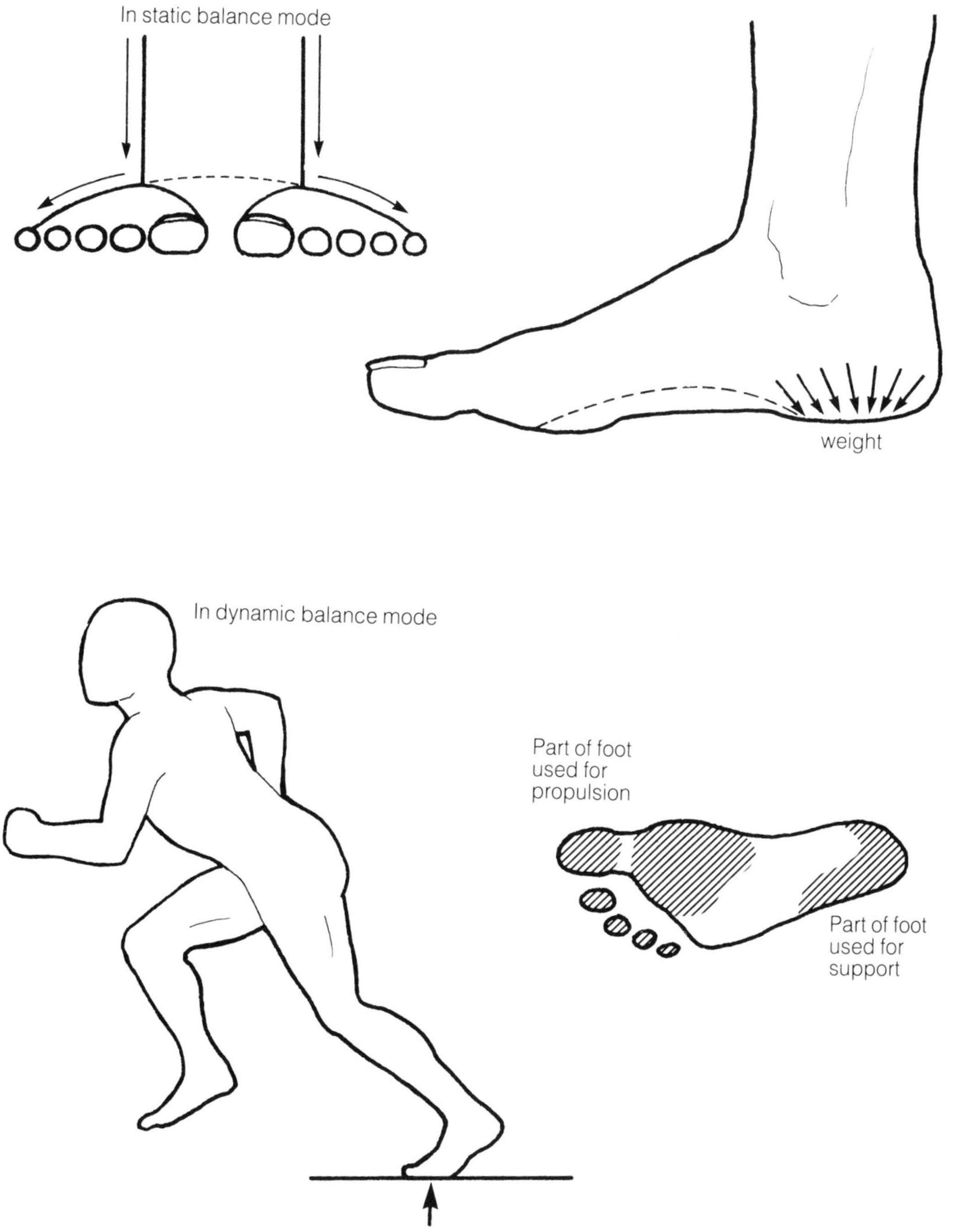

Fig 28 The foot – a supporting arch and a propulsive lever.

Fig 29 Ali Ross illustrates superb use of feet (apart) and excellent independent leg action when making athletic movements to link his turns.

stabilises the feet and prepares them for propulsive action through extension.

When you are skiing – developing athletic movements – it is natural that you use your heels for support, but in addition you must have a 'ready for action' posture which will allow you to create propulsive forces through your feet and hence your skis. These propulsive forces are used not only to step, skate and jump, but also to create the resistance to your flow which will control your direction. Your 'ready for action' posture must contain the following elements if it is to be effective.

1. Flexion of the ankles, knees and hips.
2. Legs and feet apart in order that you can use the inner edges of your feet and apply pressure through the inner edges sideways in order to deflect your flow sideways – that is, turn.
3. Independent leg action to enable you to act quickly and accurately.

In this context remember that you should always modify what you can already do in order to make progress. You do not need to learn anything new for skiing – simply modify what your body does normally when it is standing, walking, running and so on.

Fig 30 The skilled coach can 'see' the path of the centre of mass in motion. It flows across the skis as turns are linked.

Centre of Mass (Figs 30 & 31)

This is the theoretical point at which your mass can be said to be concentrated, or from which your weight acts (sometimes called the centre of gravity). Your centre of mass is an abstract concept but it can be calculated and plotted, and skilled coaches and observers can 'see' it. Skilled dancers, gymnasts and skiers can also feel it especially when in motion.

Your body shapes and movements will influence the exact position of your centre of mass but in general terms it will be in

Fig 31 Marc Girardelli (1985 World Championship silver medallist and overall World Cup winner) feels that he is 'standing' against his left (outer) foot whilst his weight acts vertically downwards.

the region of your hips, just below your navel. The centre of mass is usually slightly lower in women than in men, and it is considerably higher in young children as their trunks grow more than their legs in their early years. These differences explain why the balancing postures of women, men and children are slightly different during early skill development as skiers.

When you are moving, especially when turning, there are more forces at work than simply gravity (your weight). Weight is your perception of the force of gravity on your mass. When you are in motion you gain momentum – you have intertia. The consequence is that you feel 'heavy' in the direction of travel whenever you try to change that direction. Thus when you try to steer to the left you feel heavy downwards and in your original direction. When turning at very high speeds you will feel heavy sideways and in all turns you will feel the pressure, the forces, from the snow resistance at your skis and feet pushing sideways too. These forces act laterally and towards you in addition to gravity acting downwards. In order to balance, therefore, your centre of mass should be aligned with the resultant of all these forces. This means that it will not be vertically above your feet, although the resultant of all these forces must still pass through one of your feet. Therefore you will feel that you are standing or pressing *against* your feet rather than on them. Your legs will be inclined inwards from the arc on which you are turning.

Arms, Hands and the Hoop (Figs 32 & 33)

Imagine you are standing at the centre of a hoop which is lying on the floor. Bend down and pick it up, holding it just in front of its diameter. Notice how it influences the shape and tensions of your arms.

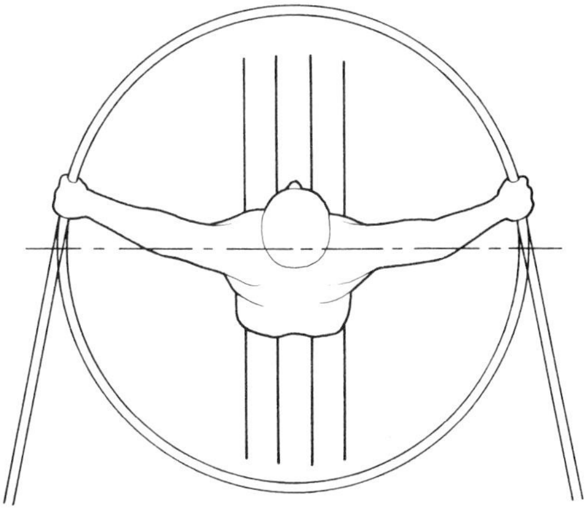

Fig 32 Hold your hoop just in front of its diameter your sticks will diverge slightly.

1. Your arms hang from your shoulders but they are alert and away from your body.
2. Your hoop tilts slightly down at the back (because of where you are holding it), so your hands hold your ski sticks pointing slightly downwards, with elbows only slightly bent.
3. The centre of your fist – your grip on the ski stick – should be in line with the big bone in your forearm. Your wrist should be 'neutral' – neither 'cocked' in, forwards or outwards.
4. You will notice that your arms are at a slight angle to your trunk. This is not a fixed angle.

In an attempt to encourage style you may be told to hold your arms and hands in a fixed shape whatever you are doing. If so, ignore such advice and read on.

The position of your arms relative to your trunk is related to the steepness of the slope and the flexion of your body. The more your upper body is inclined from the

Fig 33 Despite losing contact with the snow, Diann Roffe continued to hold an excellent hoop and went on to win the gold medal in the 1985 World Championship Giant Slalom.

vertical, the more your arms (hanging from your shoulders holding your hoop) will move away from your body. When you are skiing slowly you will only need a small hoop, but as your motion increases you will need to hold a hoop with a large diameter. As you adjust your balance, move your hoop backwards and forwards, but always keep hold of it in front of its diameter. Your ski sticks will diverge slightly.

Pelvic Tilt (Fig 34)

All your movements grow from your 'centre'. Your pelvis is the large hip bone basin at your centre, the link between your trunk and your legs and between one leg and the other. The movements of your legs and trunk are controlled by the muscles around and across your pelvis. The angle or tilt of your pelvis will influence enormously the quality of your movements.

Good dynamic balance is directly related to good posture, which arises in your lower back and depends upon good muscle tone and strength in the centre of your body. Good posture generally and vital posture when the body is in motion, is characterised by a slight upward tilt of your pelvis.

Fig 34 A slight upward tilt of his pelvis enables Marc Girardelli to maintain excellent dynamic balance at speeds in excess of seventy miles per hour.

Posture *(Fig 35)*

Good posture is the effective shape which enables you to make effective and efficient movements. In skiing, posture which will enhance your dynamic balance will exhibit all six of the factors we have just considered. Most of them are, of course, interrelated. For example, the 'hoop' and the pelvic tilt affect one another, so if your back hollows your elbows may very well pull backwards. If you stand or press too much against one heel, your pelvis will tend to tilt downwards and you will also lose some of the effective 'lean in' angle of the leg. Many changes in posture will occur when the terrain changes, but sometimes changes occur because your perception or emotional state changes, so in order to maintain control of yourself always establish a good posture.

Whenever you are showing all the six ingredients of good dynamic balancing posture, you are said to be in *neutral* posture. Dynamic balancing is best achieved with a calm mind and an alert body making positive movements athletically. When your balance is threatened always try to return to neutral before starting another movement pattern.

Fig 35 The excellent posture of Pirmin Zurbriggen shows all the features required in good dynamic balance – and enabled him to win two gold medals and one silver in the 1985 World Championships at Bormio.

Harmony

One of the characteristics of a skilful skier is that of style and elegance. Good style and elegance often give a feeling of 'quietness', of economy of movement. It would be a mistake, however, to think that the quietness and smoothness of the movements seen on the outside are in fact always felt like that by the skier. Quietness and smoothness of flow relate to your motion and not to your movements.

In order to achieve smooth flow and quiet motion you must not only make accurate and well-timed movements, but they must be made to match the terrain and the patterns of your motion. Thus you will achieve greater elegance and smoother, more skilful skiing by attending to your motion – the path of your centre of mass – as well as to your movements. In fact, when you are in open terrain it is possible that you will achieve greater skill by attending to your balance and your motion rather more than your movements. The reason for this is that when in motion on an open slope, you will never have time to respond to changes in terrain and balance when they occur. You must anticipate the line you wish to take, select a pathway and then impose a pattern – a rhythmical pattern – on your movements. The rhythm and pattern should follow the terrain and free your mind to attend to the feelings of your motion. Enjoy the sensations of motion and influence them with your movements.

Traditional Ski Instruction

One of the preoccupations of ski instructors everywhere is the technical elements which make sound movements. This is as it should be. It can, however, produce stilted movements in pupils who do not have the instructor's sense of flow. The consequence is awkward, ungraceful movements resulting in some lack of control, raised anxiety levels, frustration at not being able to ski comfortably and then a final attempt at 'posing' in order to try and look good despite it all. Of course you must learn the technical elements and modify your movements, but balance this with an awareness of motion. Cultivate the sensations of flow and resist. Feel your motion and enjoy it.

Aesthetics *(Figs 36 to 38)*

Enduring fashions and good style are founded on functionally sound movements. These can, of course, change with new equipment and evolving ski slopes which develop *pistes* from virgin snow, and moguls and ruts from smooth *pistes*, but the essential movements remain the same. Artificial style, created by skiers or instructors who wish to emphasise an aspect of ski technique for its own sake or for the sake of advertising, is, of course, legitimate in the eyes of those who 'sell' that style, but too close a pursuit by the pupil will often lead to stilted movements or even to elegant skiers who can only cope with a limited number of snow conditions in restricted terrain. The aesthetic appreciation of skiing often begins by watching better skiers, but attempts to copy often end in disappointment for the learner who remains an imitator. Deeper aesthetic appreciation arises when imitation becomes self-expression.

At the beginning of the century the simple equipment, which allowed generous movements of the feet in the boots and the boots on the skis, together with snow conditions, deep snow in open terrain, meant that the 'Arlberg crouch' was the most efficient style for speed skiing. As the boots and bindings became firmer and *pistes* were created, after ski lifts enabled thousands to ski where only dozens had previously, more upright postures emerged. During the 1960s beginners had their attention directed to the 'ideal' or 'natural' upright posture, where the weight was carried as close to the skeleton as possible. During that decade, however, the equipment and the slopes began to change again. New technology enabled skis to be made in shorter lengths, and better facilities enabled many more skiers to ski close to the flow line of the hill and so moguls appeared all over the ski slopes. At the turn of the decade Georges Jubert, the celebrated French author and genius, advocated *'avalement'* and, in his tracks, Professor Stefan Kruckenhauser of Austria proposed *'wellen'* technique as a solution to skiing in harmony with the moguls. The commercial attraction of 'unified instructional method' meant that everyone now had to crouch whether they wanted to ski moguls or not.

To the purists, who had been trying to stand upright with their feet locked together, the arrival of the *avalement* and *wellen* was seen as an ugly intrusion onto the ski slopes. The lower, slightly crouched body shape, with feet apart, appeared very objectionable. 'It will never catch on' and 'it may be fast, but I don't like the look of it' were typical comments which heralded the arrival of the 'new' technique. But aesthetic appreciation

Fig 36 Aesthetic appreciation should consider the movements and their functions in motion.

is based on more than the shape of the body. The viewer should consider the movements and their functions in motion. Efficiency, effectiveness, fluency, rhythm and control contribute to the overall impression. It soon became clear that this new technique was extremely efficient and effective in coping with the problems posed by the changing terrain. It is my opinion that any technique used simply for its own sake may appear ugly or awkward if it does not relate to the terrain in which it is being used.

Many skiers still comment that they find this or that technique unattactive, but on closer investigation I have found that such skiers are judging the skier and his technique in isolation. Aesthetic appreciation will almost certainly change if you view the techniques of skiing not as isolated movements but as a relationship between movements, motion and mountain, between the skier and the terrain. Appreciation of elegance and style in this

Fig 37 Be aware of your partner – the mountain – and aim for flow in harmony with the terrain and with your own feelings for self-expression.

manner is enhanced when you acquire the ability to use a variety of techniques in open terrain.

When skiing, instead of performing a 'solo dance' you must become aware of your partner – the mountain and hillside. The transference of attention from yourself to your partner is a considerable step forward in skill development and it requires a reasonable level of competence before it can be attempted with success. Aim for it in your own skiing because the rewards of total, harmonious co-operation with a partner can be far more satisfying and exciting than pure self-expression, however competent that might be.

The dance teacher Valerie Dunlop has said that unlike an artist who sees his work as an audience does, the dancer feels his whilst the audience *sees* what he is doing. How true this is of pupils and instructors in ski groups! The skier and the dancer have

Fig 38 Never try to adopt the correct 'position' – enjoy the dance for pleasure of the sensations of movements in motion, and not for the way it looks to others.

kinaesthetic sensations which the 'audience' can only recognise in terms of their personal memories. 'This duality is unique to movement, dance and mime and has even led to some doubt that "dances" should ever be watched. The onlooker cannot fully appreciate the muscular-nervous *experience* of the performer, but only the shapes and patterns.' (Valerie Dunlop 1963.) Until skiers and many instructors can relate the movements and innovations of top performers to their own experiences, such movements will often appear strange, sometimes even ugly. But persevere and eventually your skill will be felt for what it is: a harmony of movements and motion which partner the mountainside in a new form of folk dance. A dance which is being performed for the pleasure it gives you and not for the way it looks to others. It has been a failing of many commercial ski schools and instructional systems that they have spent more time teaching pupils to adopt the 'correct position' in order to try to look good rather than teaching them to move well and enjoy the sensations of movements in motion.

4 Improving your Skill

In Chapter 2 I recommended that you use a dry ski slope to introduce yourself to skiing. You can often do this locally and relatively cheaply, before you go to the mountains. You may, of course, continue to ski at a dry slope and never go to the snow-covered hills in winter. It is possible to ski to very high levels on dry ski slopes, but to limit yourself to them would be to miss the main point of skiing. The ultimate, perhaps, in human movements, of high-speed motion powered only by gravity and your own muscles through what is arguably the most spectacular scenery in the world. If the descent of a high Alp in deep powder snow is the dream that brings you to the beginners' slopes then the dry ski slope will awaken you with a bump. Even the nursery slopes of an Alpine village seem far removed from your dream when you begin to ski – feeling 'trapped' in heavy, stiff boots with long awkward 'feet'.

It is time then to examine your feelings and take positive action to overcome the anxiety that you are likely to feel. You may be anxious because of the lack of control you have over your equipment and because of the unfamiliarity of trying to control yourself on a tilted, slippy 'world'. This will soon be overcome if you are patient and stay on gentle slopes and run out onto level terrain. You may also feel silly and feel that everyone is looking at you and comparing you with Marc Girardelli or Ingemar Stenmark. Forget it! Everyone else is either in the same boat or has been. Being in a class will put you in the company of similar skiers and give you support. As soon as you begin to take responsibility for your own learning you will become enthralled with your own movements and problems and forget everyone else anyway. You are skiing for fun, so have fun, and if your antics give others amusement and entertainment, so much the better. You can laugh with them and appreciate their feelings too.

It is possible that you will have some anxiety about falling or injuring yourself. If you follow your instructor's advice together with my hints you should develop into a very safe skier. Modern release bindings hold your boots firmly to your skis preventing premature release if you hit bumps when skiing, but almost certainly releasing in a fall should the torque on your legs rise to a potentially dangerous level. Of course, you need to have your bindings adjusted by an expert in the ski shop and you should check the settings yourself everyday. Now that skiing is so popular you stand a greater risk of injury through a collision with other skiers than you do in a fall. For this reason, I draw your attention to the ski-way code in Chapter 5. Act positively in accordance with the code and any concern that you may have of injuring yourself will soon disappear, allowing you to get on with enjoying your learning and your sliding.

Begin at the Beginning *(Fig 39)*

I have said several times that you must take responsibility for your own learning. You have joined a ski lesson to be taught how to ski. True, but remember that although your ski instructor can ski very well indeed he cannot do it for you. Only you can do it – for you! Your ski instructor will tell you what to do; I will give you additional hints and reasons, but *you* have to do the learning. Learning takes time. Be patient and remember the principles of learning from Chapter 2 and the objectives from Chapter 1. These objectives and learning attitudes will form the foundations of your skiing career. Make them strong and work at them with confidence and positive commitment and you will make sound progress, limited only by your opportunities to ski.

The rest of this chapter will lead you through a developing pattern of movements in motion which form the essential 'thread' of all ski instruction. My suggestions may differ in small details from advice that you may receive on any single, specific occasion, but the advice which follows is based entirely on your needs. You should consider *all* instructions that you are given against this background and decide for yourself how to interpret your ski instructor's advice. My advice here applies equally to learning to ski on dry slopes as on the snow in the mountains, so take this book with you to the slopes and keep working at the basic objectives.

One word of caution. If you complete a series of lessons on a dry slope and then go to the mountains to follow it up – be modest, at least until you have adjusted to the snow and the altitude. If you have done your fitness training you will be well prepared but remember that you will travel a great deal further on every descent in the mountains than you will at the dry slope centre. Also snow is more slippery. This makes it easier to slide and to turn but it also means that you will slide more quickly and accelerate more easily. Give yourself time to get used to the 'whiteness' as well and learn to read the terrain. Study it closely and approach it with confidence but also with humility and respect.

Objective 1

Dominate your equipment.

You are in charge!

Objective 2

Be versatile.

Develop a wide repertoire of movements.

Principles of Learning

1 Do what you can do.

2 *Modify* it slightly.

3 *Repeat* your successes.

4 Attend to the *feedback* from your senses: see, hear and feel what you are doing.

Fig 39

Assessing the Slope (Fig 40)

You can try this 'game' on dry or snow slopes. It will provoke your judgement of gradient and slipperiness and enable you to assess the slope you are on, and subsequently all slopes, most accurately.

Find a level run-out area and place a marker (a twig or a hat) on this level area. Sidestep uphill to a point you judge to be high enough to enable you to run down from and just reach your marker with the tips of your skis. Feel as you slide downwards how fast you are going. How far will you slide? How close were your ski tips to your target? Keep adjusting your starting point until you achieve 'three inch' accuracy. Now try to reach your target, your marker, with the toes of your ski boots – first time! Try this every day when you first go out onto the slope and you will soon learn to judge the snow conditions and the terrain very accurately.

FOUNDATIONS

If you follow this advice and the other hints in this chapter you will build very solid foundations for your skiing career. As in all buildings, if you are aiming high then you build your foundations as deep and as solid as you can, and the building – your learning – will progress onwards and

Fig 40 In addition to the gradient of the slope you should always assess the texture and nature of its surface. Stay out of the rough, 'unpisted' snow on the right, and aim to ski on the smoother 'pisted' snow which is safer and easier to move about on.

upwards steadily and without any need to keep readjusting or redesigning the basic ingredients.

Schussing: Learning to Flow *(Fig 41)*

In ski school classes you will spend some time on schussing but probably not as much as you should. Practise as much as you can between lessons on the same safe run-out terrain that your instructor chose for you. Basic posture is learned in your early schusses and should be practised conscientiously.

1. As you flex at the knees and ankles, your shins incline forwards. Always move your shoulders down forwards too so that your back is more or less parallel with your lower legs.
2. Once you start moving keep your trunk flexed at the hips so that your upper body is always inclined as much or more than your shins.
3. Start sliding with your skis hip-width apart. *Ignore* any advice to clamp your feet or skis close together – even if it does appear that some skiers do that.
4. Feel your skis running flat on their soles. Steer them straight by pointing your

Fig 41 'Now look down at your skis!'

Fig 42 During your first few descents, crouch but keep your shoulders in front of your feet.

feet and your knees in the direction you want the skis to slide.

5. 'Now look down at your skis!' You may be told not to do this, so I had better explain why you should. Look down at your skis to see if they are doing what you intend them to do and what you feel they are doing. This visual feedback will enable you to learn how to steer them and how tc feel them more accurately and so reinforce your kinaesthetic learning. Now look ahead and watch where you are going. You need to watch the terrain and where you are going very carefully. Nevertheless, on smooth slopes glancing at your skis occasionally will help you to learn more quickly how to feel what they are doing and what you are doing to control them. Use your eyes to tell you what you need to know in order to learn but remember that you must, with practice and patience, learn to *feel* what your body movements are, be aware of your motion and watch where you are going – precisely.

Coping with Speed (Fig 42)

A normal human movement to cope with speed and accelerating forces is to crouch. During your first few schusses you feel that you are sliding quite quickly – so crouch. As you learn to slide freely, to flow down the hill, gradually stand more erect and keep your crouch in reserve for higher speeds later on.

Athletic Movements
(Figs 43 & 44)

During your first few descents you will probably keep quite still and try to imitate the posture and shape of your ski instructor – or simply 'freeze' because it seems the simplest thing to do. Refined movements follow later when you feel familiar and comfortable with sliding – with flowing freely downhill onto a safe run-out area.

When you have confidence that you can steer your skis parallel to each other and in a straight line it is time to remember the objectives from Chapter 1: to dominate your equipment and develop full control over yourself. You will be instructed to 'bend your knees' or 'bend your ankles' and doing so will enable you to achieve a good basic posture. More important however is what you use that posture for! The basic posture is one of readiness for athletic movement.

1. Bend your ankles, but straighten them too. Feel your calves press on the *back* of your boots as well as feeling for your shins on the tongue of the boot.
2. By extending and flexing at the ankles more and more rapidly you will soon be able to spring lightly and even hop – landing gently. You are simply regaining, in ski boots and in motion, the ability to skip that you had immediately before you put on the ski boots.
3. A variation on this theme is to try and

Fig 43 'Bend your knees' in order to be able to spring lightly. Try springing, with good ankle extension, over lines or markers on the slope to improve the accuracy and timing of your movements.

shoot your feet ahead of you and then pull them back underneath you again.

4. Keep hold of your hoop!

5. In every springy movement you make remember to keep your trunk inclined forwards. We call this keeping the hip-angle *'closed'*. It is an important feature of good dynamic balance.

6. Now develop a wide variety of movements which test your balance and your steering ability whilst you slide downhill.

7. With confidence and sensitivity for feeling the inside of your feet, you will learn that your skis can grip the snow. This will enable you to step sideways whilst flowing downhill and eventually to turn out of the flow line and run to a halt. Step and run as lightly as you can, using your feet and ankles athletically.

Fig 44 When you enjoy 'flowing' you can learn to schuss like the top downhill racers. Here, Franz Klammer the world's greatest downhill racer demonstrates the essentials of the racing tuck: (a) skis apart and flat on the slope; (b) knuckles together; (c) elbows in front of your knees; (d) back parallel to the slope.

Falling *(Figs 45 & 46)*

Everyone falls, some more often than others it is true. Falling can be uncomfortable on dry slopes but it is all part of the fun in soft snow. When you feel you have lost balance and a fall is inevitable a couple of dos and don'ts will keep you safe.

1. Try to avoid falling forwards, as you have further to fall if you do.
2. Hold your sticks firmly – *do not* let go of your grip. This will protect your fingers and thumbs.
3. Try to sit down just to the side of your skis and just before you reach the slope. *Straighten your legs* firmly and decisively. This action will ensure that your legs do not twist. It also has the added benefit of causing you to turn on the hill and usually brings your skis to rest below you and across the flow line, making it easier for you to stand up again.

Fig 45 When you 'sit' down to the side, both you and your skis still have forward momentum. Notice how this girl's knee has dug in the snow and acted as a pivot around which her momentum has caused her to twist. To avoid the danger in this sort of fall, always straighten your legs before you hit the slope.

Fig 46 Always straighten your legs if you fall.

Standing Again

Before you try to stand up again, spend a minute or two getting your breath back. Do a quick check to see that you and all your equipment are all right and reassure your friends that you are not hurt.

1. Look down the slope and ensure your skis are parallel and across the flow line.
2. Sit close to your feet, move your head and shoulders over your feet – chest as close to your knees as you can – and then stand up, pushing against the edges of your skis and using your hands or ski sticks to give you a lift.
3. If you have difficulty in standing up again, just ask anyone nearby to give you a hand. They will be glad to oblige, having been in the same situation themselves perhaps. It gets easier with practice and is easier still on steeper slopes.
4. If you should lose your skis in a fall, collect them and put the upper ski on first if you are on a slope. Turn around and then put the other upper one on.

Fig 47 If you have difficulty balancing during your first few descents, your instructor may support you like this. This can be good fun if you practise with a friend.

Developing Flow *(Fig 47)*

During the first few hours on skis you should be learning what the skis do – how they slide and how the edges grip. When you move, walking or schussing, steer your skis with your feet and slide them rather than lift them whenever you can. During your early descents you will be experiencing pure flow, balancing on sliding skis with gravity doing most of the work. You will feel at times like a passenger on long creatures that have minds of their own. After twenty or thirty descents you should have enough control of your movements and your equipment to begin to *modify* what your skis are doing as they slide straight down.

LEARNING TO RESIST
(Figs 48 to 50)

After several hours of schussing you are confident and beginning to show good signs of athletic movements whilst you flow directly down the slope. In order to progress towards your dream – the descent of the high mountains – you will need to be able to control and direct your flow. You can do this by resisting it. By creating appropriate resistance selectively, you can balance flow and resistance so that you steer your skis where you want them to go, controlling both speed and direction.

Gravity pulls you and your skis down your flow line. Gravity is the source of our motive power. How then can we steer on skis? Your skis will only deviate from the flow line if they are pushed by a sideways force, which offers some resistance to your forward motion. This resistance or deflecting force arises in the snow or the matting. It is not friction, which is the 'stickiness' of the sliding surface, but an adjustable resistance which is caused by two factors:

1. The angle of your skis in relation to your direction of travel.
2. The design characteristics, the flex, shaping and torsional rigidity of your skis.

Fig 48 By using the design of the ski and by pushing it firmly sideways and down into the snow (or matting) the deformed ski will steer around an arc.

To steer your skis you must learn to use these two factors.

The second factor, the design features of the skis, is, of course, the more difficult to use, but only because of the accuracy needed in your movements. This will improve with practice and most quickly if you understand and can feel for what you are trying to achieve.

Your skis are both wider and more flexible at the tip and tail than they are under foot. This means that the tip and tail can grip the snow when the ski is 'edged' (tilted) and the ski can then be deformed into an arc like a bow. The tip area of the ski, the shovel as it is known, bends the most and will lead the ski along an arc or curving track (*see Fig 48*). Putting the ski on edge alone will not make it deform into an arc. In fact, an edged ski will run in a straight line if it is of the right stiffness for your weight. How then do you deform the ski into an arc? How do you press it into *reverse camber*? This can be done by either dropping onto it quickly or by extending your leg rapidly – either way will produce reverse camber but only for a very short time. These methods are used by slalom racers occasionally when they need a short, sharp 'carve', but will not enable you to sustain a curved ski to steer with.

The way to deform your ski is very simple if you consider what happens when you are

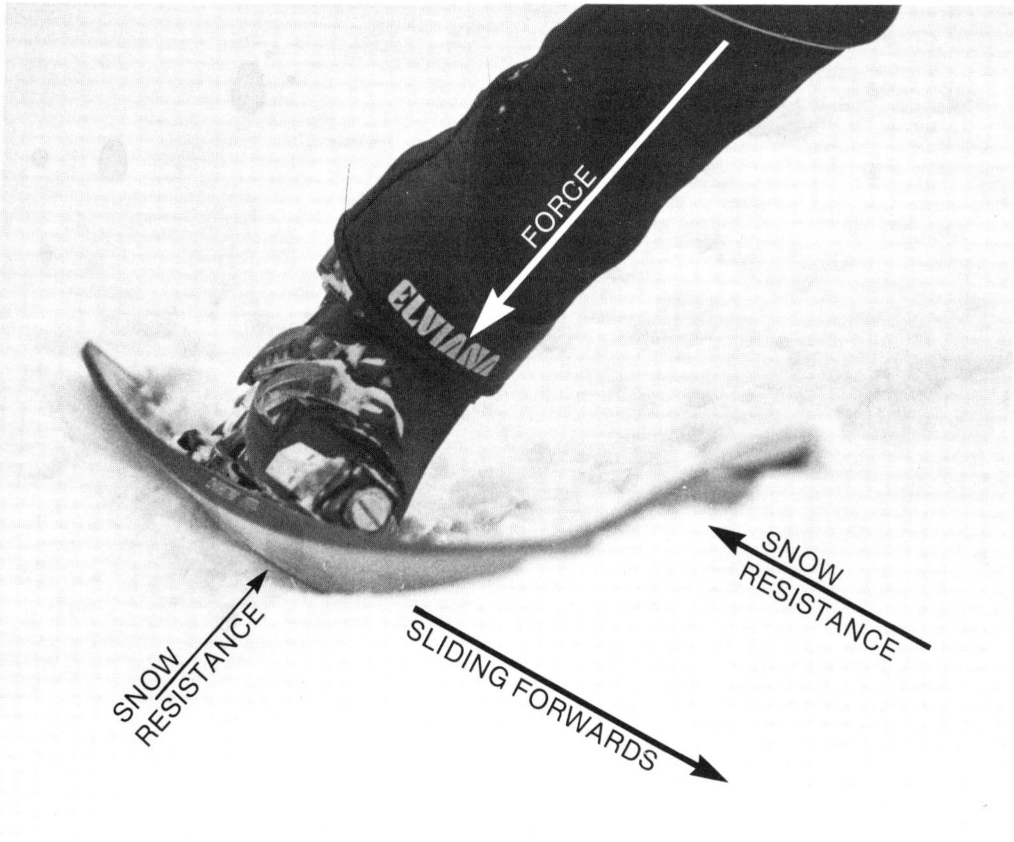

Fig 49 Using resistance and the design features of a ski to steer very accurately.

in motion. Gravity causes you to slide downhill, but when you are in motion you have inertia. This is the tendency to keep going in a straight line. You know this as your momentum, a product of your mass and your velocity (speed in a straight line), and feel it as your flow. If your skis are apart, they are slightly out to either side of your centre of mass – the centre or focus for your inertia. If you now turn one leg inwards slightly the tip of the ski moves in line with your inertia, and if you are pressing on your toe the wider shovel area of that edged and turned ski will meet some resistance as it tries to go sideways in the snow. The ski thus grips at the front, and because your foot is attached in the middle, the ski you are now standing *against* deforms into an arc and helps you to steer along a curved path.

The accuracy of movement required to steer very smoothly will come with practice, but to start with you need to get the feeling of simply turning your skis at an angle to the direction of your flow and feeling the resistance that you can create by this action. Turning your skis at an angle to your flow causes them to skid. Steering your skidding is how you control your flow. All turning on skis contains an element of skidding, more or less depending upon the mix of ingredients in your movements.

The attempt to steer skis without any skidding, by using only the design characteristics of the skis is called *carving*. This is an important action to aim for when you become expert, but in reality very few pure carved turns ever occur. The value of the carved turn is as an idea that helps you to understand how the skis can work for you and how their design can influence what happens after you have turned the skis at angles to your direction of flow.

The first step in learning to control your flow so that eventually you will be able to direct it and thus steer is learning to resist your flow, down the same gentle slope that you have been practising on so far. You will learn the sensations of resisting your flow most easily by turning both skis at an angle to your flow line – symmetrically. This action is called ploughing or snow-ploughing.

Fig 50 Franz Klammer demonstrates how to learn 'resisting' by simply modifying a basic schuss.

Fig 51 The snow resistance will force your skis back into the flow line unless you push them out sideways as your turn them.

PLOUGHING *(Fig 51)*

Learning to plough is the biggest single 'step' you will make in learning to ski. It involves movements and sensations which are quite different from everyday walking, yet it is the basis for most of your advanced skiing if you can learn to do it well. If you base your learning method on what you know and then modify this to produce new movements and new motion, you will find ploughing very simple.

1. Schuss down the slope with your skis hip-width apart or slightly wider – never narrower. You have at this stage developed good ankle and knee articulation, good dynamic balance, confidence and a measure of athleticism. You are prepared to plough.
2. Whilst sliding downhill crouch a little.
3. Steer your skis a little wider apart then turn your toes and ski tips inwards slightly. As soon as you do this the extra resistance against the tilted soles of the skis will force them back into the flow line. To plough and therefore to resist effectively you must now push the skis out sideways as you turn the tips inwards slightly. This is very easy and can be done using either of two techniques. It does not matter which technique you use first but you must learn and practise both if you are to build solid foundations for your future progress. The first method of creating the 'pushing out' forces is by using your weight, the second is by using your muscles and your leg strength. Both methods are valuable but the weight method is probably easier to begin with until you develop the feeling of ploughing.

Weight Method *(Fig 52)*

1. As soon as you begin to steer your skis apart and turn your legs, you should simply bend a little lower and 'sag' between your skis. Try to imagine that your weight is flowing downwards through bending legs. Make yourself 'heavy' in your hips and trunk.
2. Maintain good basic posture and lower your arms and hands as well as your hips.
3. The key sensations here are bending legs and a sagging feeling.

Fig 52 The weight method of ploughing. The key sensations are bending legs and heaviness or sagging in the hips and trunk.

If you find this difficult to do whilst sliding forwards, try to make these movements before you start, supported by your sticks. Then push yourself to start with your sticks.

Strength Method *(Fig 53)*

To achieve ploughing this way is only slightly more difficult than by sagging or using your weight to push your skis apart, but it is much more useful in the long term as it is more controllable and has the added advantage of generating an active feeling of resistance under your feet.

1. Schuss with your skis wider than hip-width apart. This is so that you can feel the inside edges of your feet and skis.
2. Crouch down quite low, keeping good basic posture and with ankles, as well as knees, flexed.
3. Turn the ski tips inwards and at the same time push your feet apart, against the balls of your feet, by extending your legs.
4. As you push the snow or matting sideways you will feel the resistance you are generating. You will probably slow down a little too.
5. By relaxing or 'softening' your legs the snow will push your skis into the flow line again and if you keep slightly crouched your legs will bend.
6. Extend and push out again without standing upwards; play about with these movements of push and bend alternately.

Now that you can plough, return to the basic objectives and learn to dominate your equipment and yourself by trying a variety of activities whilst ploughing down the flow line.

1. Maintain ploughing and develop good ankle and knee flexion and extension.
2. Develop these movements until you can spring lightly off the balls of your feet – keeping good posture with your hip angle closed.

You are now ploughing athletically and are ready to combine the two techniques to enable you to plough more comfortably and more skilfully.

As you slide downhill begin ploughing by using your leg extension and then maintain the plough by relaxing your hips and allowing your weight to do the work. You can now plough with an almost effortless feeling. From this basic plough you can bring leg work into play and push your feet out or pull them in at will.

Practise repeatedly changing the angle and the width of your plough and learn to feel what you are doing and how you are doing it. *Feedback* will help here.

1. Listen to the sounds of your skis as you push them and slide them.
2. Watch your skis – when you have a safe run-out area ahead of you – let your eyes tell your legs what they are doing until they can feel it for themselves.

Your ski instructor may tell you never to look down at your skis. What he really means is that you should look ahead to see the terrain and where you are going rather than stare at your ski tips. It is however perfectly normal for you to want to look at your skis – mainly for the visual feedback. To avoid looking at your skis (except when you want feedback from your movements) and to watch where you are going further ahead, you have to learn what the terrain and your motion feels like and then predict with your eyes what the terrain will be like to ski on, and feel if you are right. Once you are able to predict how the skis will behave, you will no longer need to look down at them.

Fig 53 The strength method of ploughing. Feel how you can push the skis apart by extending your legs away from your centre.

Here is a little game to aid this aspect of your learning. Place a marker on the run-out of the slope as you did earlier and keep your eyes on it as you plough towards it. Stop with your ski tips just touching the marker. Now repeat the same thing and close your eyes during the descent. *Feel* for good posture, good balance and the resistance at your feet and judge when you are at the marker. Open your eyes when you stop.

You are now able to flow and resist and no doubt want to get on with learning more advanced manoeuvres. It is good that you are so enthusiastic and it is perfectly normal for you to want to progress as quickly as possible. Be patient! By all means try and move on but keep returning to and practising these variations of ploughing and schussing. Change from one to the other during a single descent. In this way you will build your foundations as solidly as possible and prepare yourself to move on in such a way that you only need make small, continuing modifications in order to make progress. The basis of all the progress you make from now on will be sound preparation and small, continuing modifications.

SKIDDING AND STEERING *(Fig 54)*

Whenever you are ploughing, your skis are skidding. They are pointed or turned at an angle to their motion. If a ski is skidding completely broadside on to its motion, it is obviously meeting much more resistance than if it is only travelling slightly sideways in relation to its direction of travel. There is therefore a continuum or spectrum of all shades of skidding from completely *raw* skidding to absolutely *pure* carving. Where you are on this continuum, i.e. how much steering you effect, will depend upon how much and how quickly you turn your skis across their direction of motion and also how much they are edged. At the pure end of this spectrum (carving) there is no skidding – the ski travels along its own length, deformed in reverse camber (arc). Moving down the spectrum there is some skidding with the skis tending to 'grip' more at the shovels than at the rails. While at the raw end (skidding) the skis are broadside on to your motion or momentum.

How much? How quickly? How edged? By experimenting with these three factors in respect of turning the skis across your motion, you will begin to develop the ability to steer your skis.

1. Schuss downhill and then plough with one leg and ski. If you have good balance you should be able to feel the resistance building against that ski as it skids.
2. Sink down to consolidate your balance and your ability to push. Push now against the skidding ski (without moving your hips from the centre).
3. Push more by extending the ploughing leg. As you feel the resistance against this ski you will also notice that you are being deflected from your original flow line.

Another way to achieve a deflection is by edging one ski more than the other whilst ploughing. To edge efficiently, move your *thigh* inwards. If you move only your knee in (as many instructors demand) then you run the risk of turning your hips or moving them sideways over your ski. This will reduce the effect of edging and cause your thigh to rotate, which could be dangerous and which is certainly inefficient as far as control of your edge is concerned.

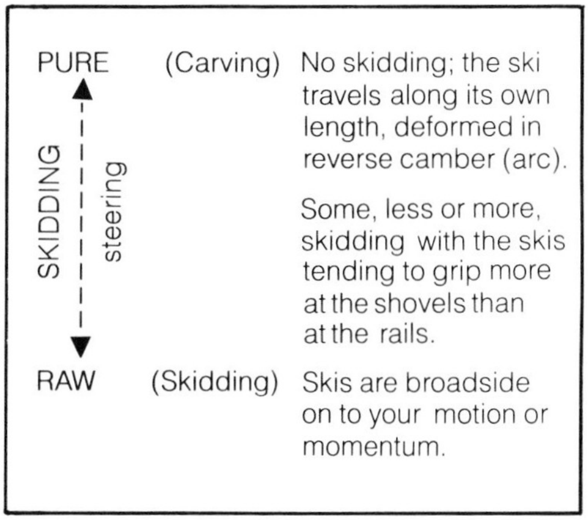
PURE
(Carving)
No skidding; the ski travels along its own length, deformed in reverse camber (arc).
SKIDDING
steering
Some, less or more, skidding with the skis tending to grip more at the shovels than at the rails.
RAW
(Skidding)
Skis are broadside on to your motion or momentum.

Fig 54 The spectrum of skidding.

'To edge – move one thigh in.'

1. After moving one thigh in, return to neutral symmetry.
2. Repeat with your other leg.

You will find that you can now control the degree of edging and so deflect your plough – crab-like – down the hill. You are almost ready now to use the design of the ski to help you steer. But first, apply the movements that you have learned and use them to deflect your motion from the flow line as you descend.

APPLYING YOUR TECHNIQUE *(Figs 55 to 60)*

On a dry ski slope, look down and notice the matting is laid in strips. You can see seams approximately six feet apart. We call the distance between two seams 'one mat wide'. In the centre of a one mat wide strip of ski slope, begin your descent.

1. Flow down and resist by ploughing.
2. Push gently, first one ski then the other.
3. Deflect your skis from seam to seam, using a descent width of one mat wide.
4. Repeat the exercise but this time feel that you are pushing (slight leg extension) against the edge of your ski – first one then the other. You can deflect your flow rhythmically, from side to side – one mat wide. Practise this during several descents, making sure you can do it with good rhythm and varying tempos. You can even vary the rhythm during one descent – slow, slow, quick, quick, slow and so on.
5. Now you are ready to use the design of your skis to help you steer. Steering is achieved by applying pressure between skis and snow or matting. This pressure or resistance to motion can, as we have seen, be achieved in two ways: using weight by bending, or muscles by extending. You will use both of these in sequence to create a continuous pressure between the skis and snow and thus steer them precisely where you want them to go.
6. Descend the flow line in a narrowish, comfortable plough. Deflect from seam to seam – one mat wide.
7. After four or five deflections using one mat wide, aim to steer your plough up to but still between the seams two mats wide.

This change in task will demand and so cause a change in technique – a small modification of your movements.

1. As your plough crosses the flow line, allow your legs to bend and your upper body to flow over your outer ski. Your body will flex at your hips and bend forwards, allowing your head to move over and towards the forebody of your outer ski. Your weight is now pressing against an edged and turning ski and its design will

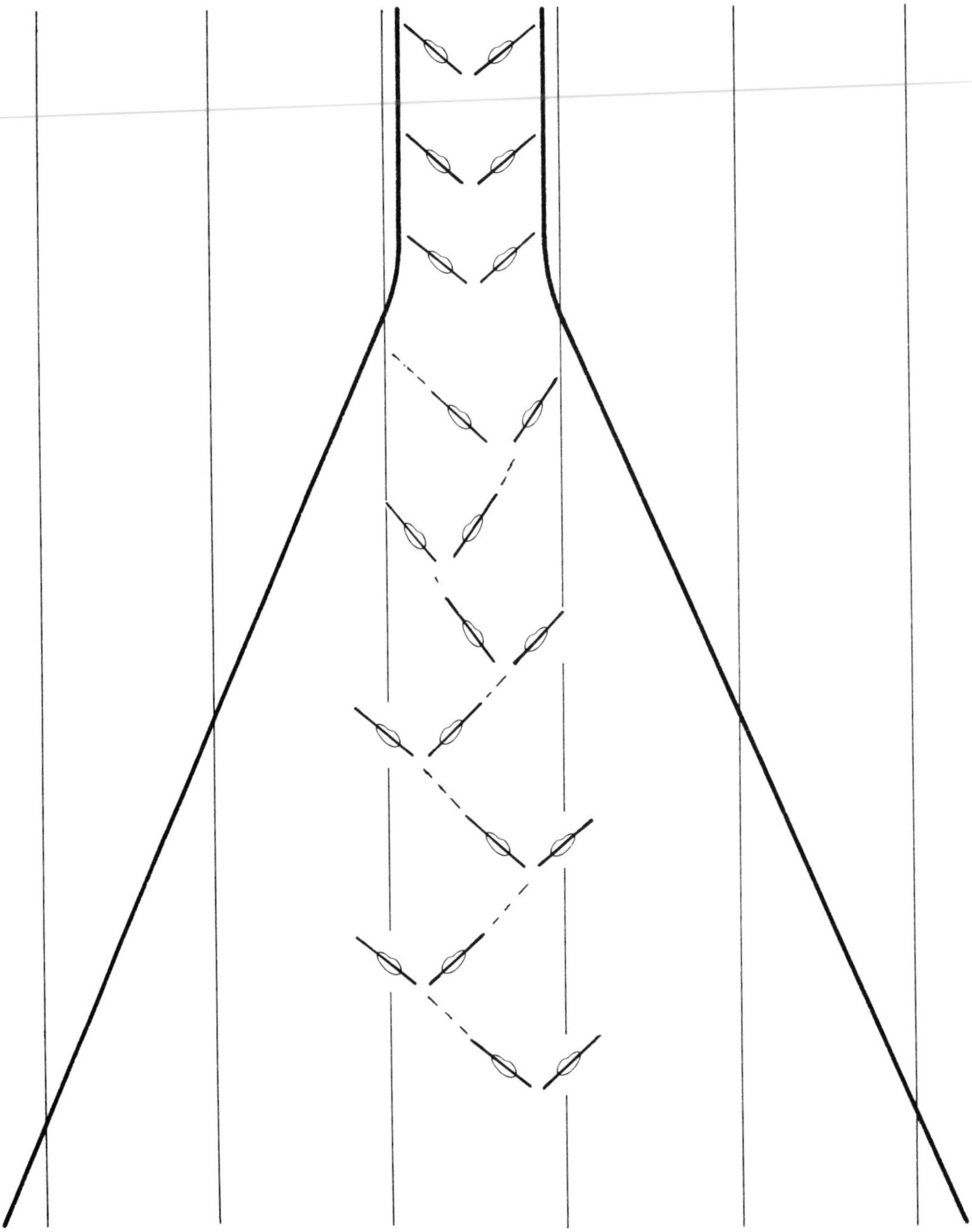

Fig 55 The funnel – superimposed on the seams of the matting on a dry ski slope. Deflect your plough – crab-like – from seam to seam until your feet touch the seams one mat wide.

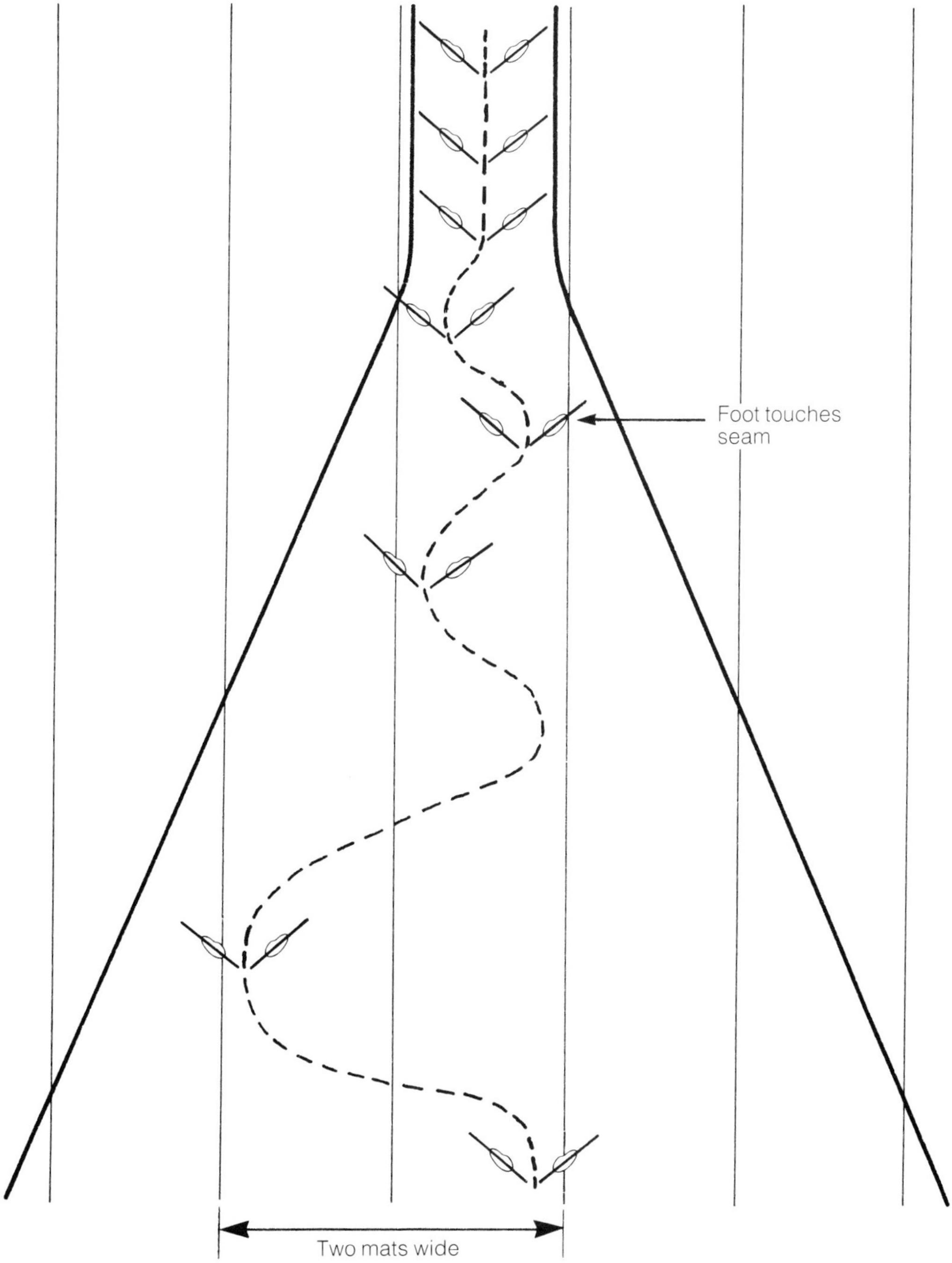

Fig 56 By changing your task – steering from one mat wide to two mats wide – you will demand a small change in your movements, in your technique. Your motion will have an effect on your movements.

Fig 57 As your plough crosses your flow line, allow your upper body to continue to flow and so bend slightly at the hips over the front of the outer ski. (Do not bend sideways at the waist.) By allowing your momentum to flow in this manner your mass in motion brings your weight to bear against your edged outer ski which will now skid slightly and steer around the turn.

Fig 58 As your speed increases and you steer from seam to seam two mats wide, add muscle power to your weight in order to steer more accurately. To steer your plough towards the flow line, extend your outer leg and press against your 'big toe'. Allow your momentum (upper body) to flow only after you have begun to turn.

steer you around the turn.
2. Stay low, crouched slightly, and steer your plough into the next turn by using your muscle power. Extend your (new) outer leg and push against the instep of your foot. As you feel the snow or mat resisting you will steer yourself across the flow line. As your ski crosses your flow line, soften your outer leg, grip with the edge of the ski and allow your hips to flex and your upper body to bend towards the outer ski.

This action is *appropriate angulation*, a fundamental movement to control edging, steering and most of all dynamic balance when you are turning.

As you will only .be able to concentrate on one thing at a time, feel for these movements during one descent. Then, during the next descent, use these movements to control your motion; i.e. steer from seam to seam using two mats wide.

This approach to learning is very effective if you alternate your attention between task and technique – between what you want to do and how you intend to do it. Attending to the task – aiming your skis – will cause small modifications in your technique. If you attend to these movements you will be more able to solve the next task.

Develop your skill and your control over yourself and your skis by continually changing the task.

1. First turn rhythmically in one mat wide.
2. Then use two mats wide.
3. Use three mats wide.
4. Then onto four mats wide, making each turn very accurately.

If you have a long slope to practise on, use two mats, then three, then two again and onto four until you can control both the *direction* and the *speed* of your skis and of your motion.

Fig 59 It is important to ski close to your flow line and make small deflections. Feel the snow resistance and your skis working for you. Do not force your turns otherwise your movements will become awkward and very ineffective.

A Test of your Skill (Figs 61 to 63)

When you can schuss down the flow line, resist by ploughing and then steer down the funnel – controlling your speed as the slope gets steeper; then and only then have you developed the necessary foundations of *skill* which will prepare you to learn more advanced skiing.

You are now able to flow and resist. You are able to direct your flow by selective and accurate resisting and have demonstrated your ability to:

1. *Dominate* your equipment and your body movements.
2. Make a variety of movements so that you have *versatility* in the size and shapes of turns and control at various speeds on varying terrain.
3. Make small but continuing *modifications* to your movements and your motion and so progress steadily in your learning.

You have achieved the objectives we set out in Chapter 1.

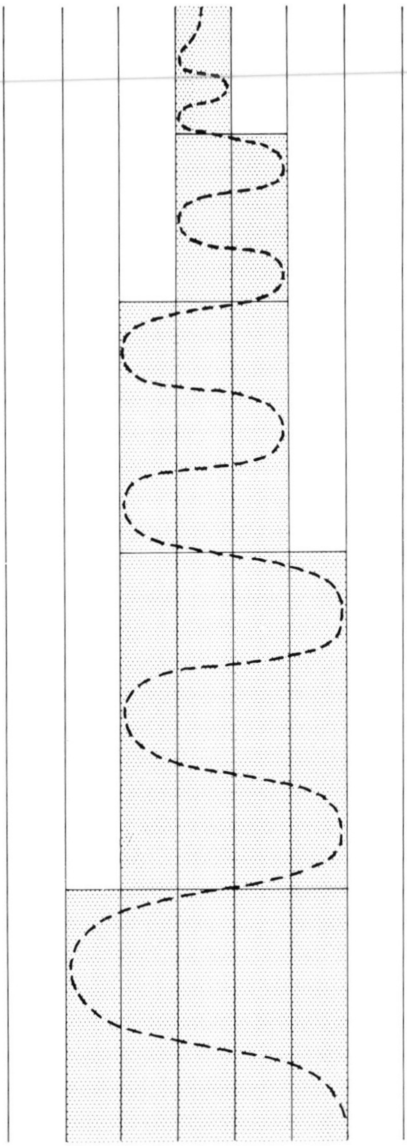

Fig 60 The funnel – a learning aid. Steer accurately, within but up to the seams of one mat wide, then two, three, four or more. On successive descents down the same slope, attend alternately to task and then technique.

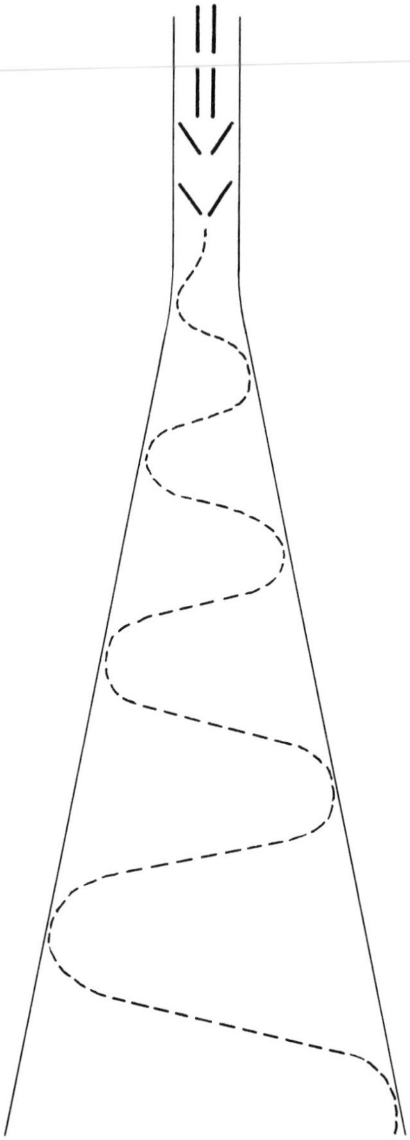

Fig 61 The funnel – a test of your skill. When you can steer to the edges of the funnel accurately and do so slowly even if the terrain gets steeper then you have learned how to control your flow by selective and directed resistance. You are now prepared to learn more advanced movements – influenced even more by your motion than you have been so far.

Fig 62 Sarah Lewis plough steering by using the strength method (leg extension to begin to turn). This method of plough steering is a sound foundation for more advanced techniques and should be practised repeatedly.

Fig 63 Morgan Jones, British Junior Champion 1984 and 1985, making a racing slalom turn. Compare this with Fig 62.

BALANCING RESISTANCE AND FLOW *(Fig 64)*

What you have been doing so far is called snowplough turning or plough steering. Your motion is well under control, but the speed is quite slow, and your movements are well controlled but also fairly slow. Accuracy of movement and aim in motion is very important, but it is now time to introduce more athletic movements and to build up patterns of movements in motion which will enable you to approach ballistic movement with control of your emotions, your perceptions and, most of all, control of your flow. You will do this by following the process we have already established, but by changing – indeed reversing – the task which you solve on the hillside.

So far you have skied down the first funnel, which brought your free flow under control, by changing your movements to solve the terrain tasks and the speed tasks. Free flow gave way to complete control of speed and direction. So much so that at the end of the first funnel, turning slowly in four or five mats wide, you could *choose*, in every turn, either to begin the next turn or traverse off the side.

Now you will use the second funnel, and in this funnel learn to use athletic movements; changing the task to move from complete control of resistance to controlled flow in rhythmically linked turns, close to the flow line but with appropriate resistance being used to deflect your flow rather than reduce it a great deal. Your objective now is to use the principles of Chapter 1 and the learning method of continuing modification in order to achieve a controlled balance between flow and resistance, in harmony with the terrain and at whatever speed of descent you wish.

Feedback and Learning

I shall here use playing darts to illustrate a method of learniing. This is based on the idea that if you attempt a task, e.g. hitting the 'twenty' on a dart board, with good feedback, then you are likely to learn more effectively than if someone, say an instructor, simply tells you what movements to make. Thus, the important ingredients when learning are:

1. What you are trying to achieve.
2. The quality of feedback when you attempt the task.
3. Small modifications of your movements whilst still attending to the main task.

It is these small modifications which I will describe here. Consider them as coaching points or hints on how to solve the task effectively.

Feedback is vital to the learning process and it usually comes from the instructor; for example, 'don't sit back' or 'bend your ankles more next time'. It might also be in the form of encouragement: 'a good attempt, now try to develop a stronger ryhthm'. In all of these examples the instructor is providing feedback. This is valuable but not as valuable as you using intrinsic feedback yourself.

Imagine you are learning to play darts. Your instructor describes the movements you should make and demonstrates how to throw the dart and hit the target. He challenges you to imitate him, but as you let go of the dart he turns out the light. He then gives you feedback, telling you if you did well or not and how to do better next time. To learn by this method would be a long slow process, likely to produce

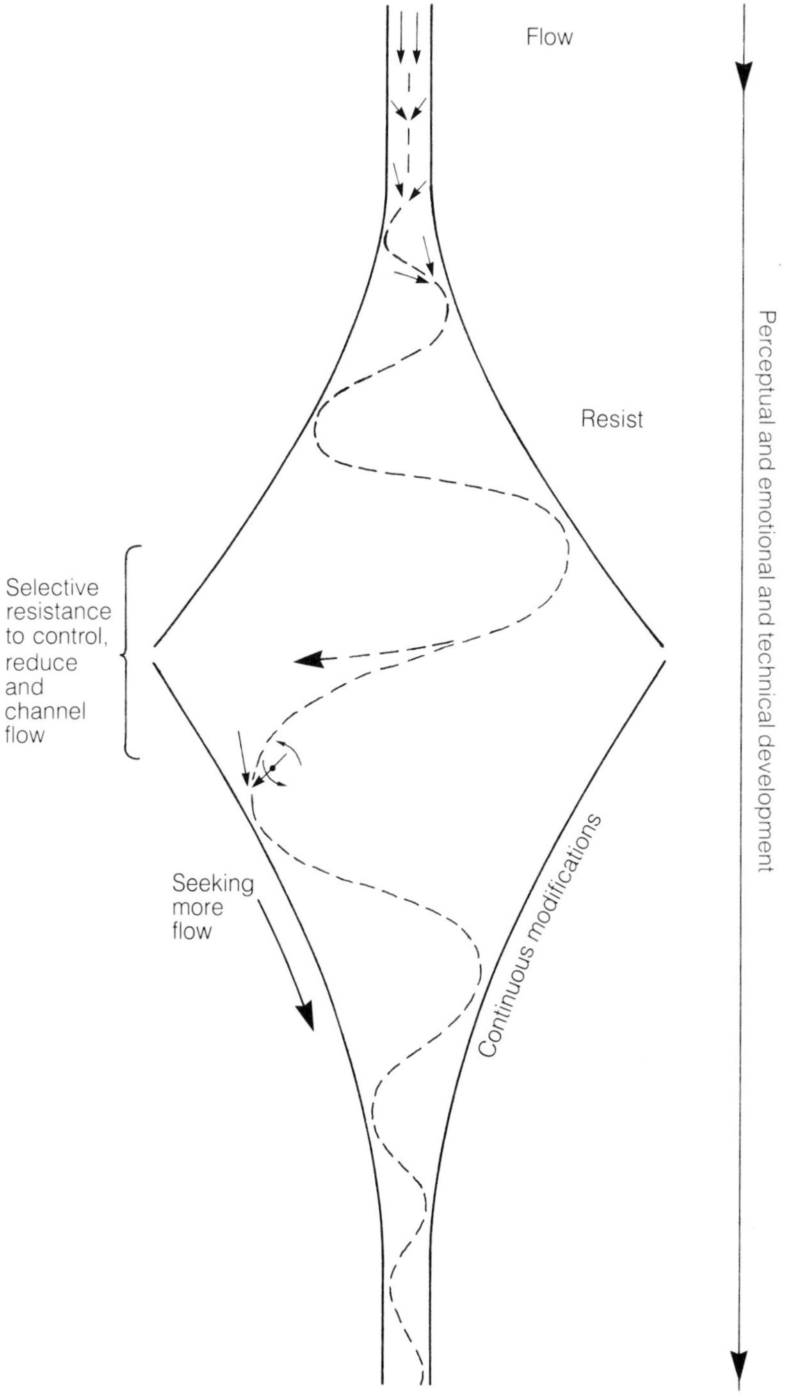

Fig 64 The funnel – extending the task by modifying the 'target' as you descend the slope.

awkward movements and a relatively low level of consistency. So it is in skiing if you use this method.

I propose, therefore, that you learn to ski using the normal darts method. This is to find a safe area to play in, with a coach or instructor telling you what to do in overall terms. Make many practice attempts, using your own intrinsic feedback. Take hints from your coach or instructor whilst you keep throwing darts at the board *feeling* what you are doing, *watching* the dart in flight and also *listening* to it landing or hitting. Very small sensitive modifications are possible by this method and so you will develop smoothly, with maximum progress, fluency of movements and satisfaction.

To use this method in skiing you have to have an objective – a task to solve – using the techniques you have at your disposal. Trying to solve a new task will cause you to develop and learn new movements. The role of the instructor or coach is to guide you through the task and help you modify your current movements so that you succeed at the new task with movements which are sound and which will build foundations. This will prepare you for further development and learning. In this way your skill as a skier will continue to expand and develop without a disheartening plateau or periods when you feel you cannot make any progress. Progress is always possible as long as you modify what you can do, rather than attempt and often fail something you cannot yet do.

Ski the Funnel *(Figs 65 to 70)*

Your next new task is to ski the second funnel. As you attempt to solve this task you will be changing your motion, which in turn will influence your movements, which will then help you to change your motion more.

The task has two parts: firstly 'ski' and secondly 'the funnel'.

1. By ski I mean flow down the hill under good control, making movements which flow one from another.
2. By the funnel I mean steer your skis from edge to edge of the funnel.

Let us look at this in practice and consider the small modifications you will make as you ski down the funnel.

1. Enter the funnel at the top. Make linked snowplough turns as you did earlier. Use four mats wide for each turn and gradually narrow the angle of your plough. You will travel quite quickly now, but still under excellent control, feeling good resistance or pressure under the outer foot as you steer to and from the seams, four mats wide. Your outer foot is your 'dart' and your dart board is four mats wide – aim for the outer edge of it but keep within it.
2. After making five or six turns aim to steer your turns to the seams three mats wide. Remember to extend the outer leg to steer downhill and then to grip with the outer foot and ski, bending against that ski as the turn progresses. Steer your outer ski very accurately to three mats wide but narrow the angle of your plough a little more.
3. After making six or eight turns assess how you feel. Are you in control of your movements, aim and emotions? Are you safe and happy, enjoying what you are doing? If the answer is 'no' then steer back to four mats wide or move to a shallower ski slope if this is possible. When you do feel happy and confident, in control of your movements and your motion, then proceed.

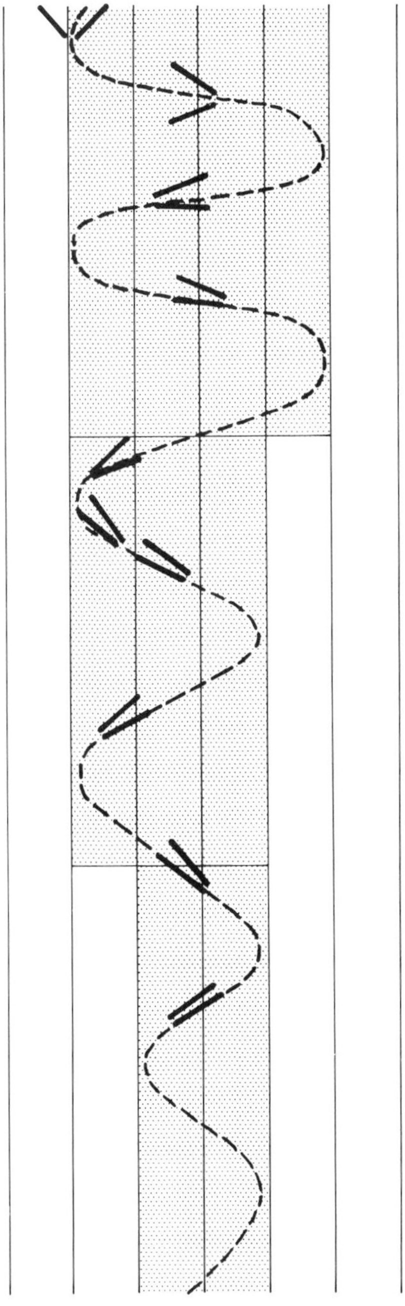

Fig 65 Ski the slope many times at four mats wide with as narrow a plough angle as you can achieve. When you are ready – feeling in control and happy with your increased flow – seek more flow within three mats wide.

4. Steer your narrow plough to the seams two mats wide. Make as many rhythmically linked turns as you can. You will now feel that you are not resisting as much as you were before – you are indeed flowing down the hillside, but still in good control. Changing the task from four through three to two mats wide has changed your motion and your movements. It is now time to make a small modification to your movements, which will in turn modify your motion again.

5. As you are steering your plough two mats wide extend the outer leg to press firmly against your outer foot as you steer downhill. As you press the outer foot bend the inner leg slightly. Keep your hip angle closed and do not stand upwards – simply move your knee towards your chest ever so slightly. This enables you to identify and slightly lift the tip of your inner ski. Repeat this rhythmically in each turn. This action was described as 'pedalling' by the Japanese Demonstration Team at Interski, Sexton, in 1983.

6. When you have established these movements with good rhythm and accuracy, move into a one mat wide band of matting or snow. As you ski down one mat wide try to actively seek more flow. Maintain your rhythm and accuracy of skis – keep turning a full one mat wide but add powerful, athletic leg movements – starting with your ankles – and try to go downhill as fast as you feel comfortable. Enjoy the flow.

It is probable that you are now skiing in a manner which looks as if you are making skilfully linked parallel turns, but there is still one small modification to make.

7. Each time you bend your inner leg and lift the ski tip, *turn* your inner leg so that the tip of your inner ski moves *away* from the

Fig 66 Once you are confident that you can ski the funnel accurately, speed up your motion by narrowing your plough even more and by speeding up your movements.

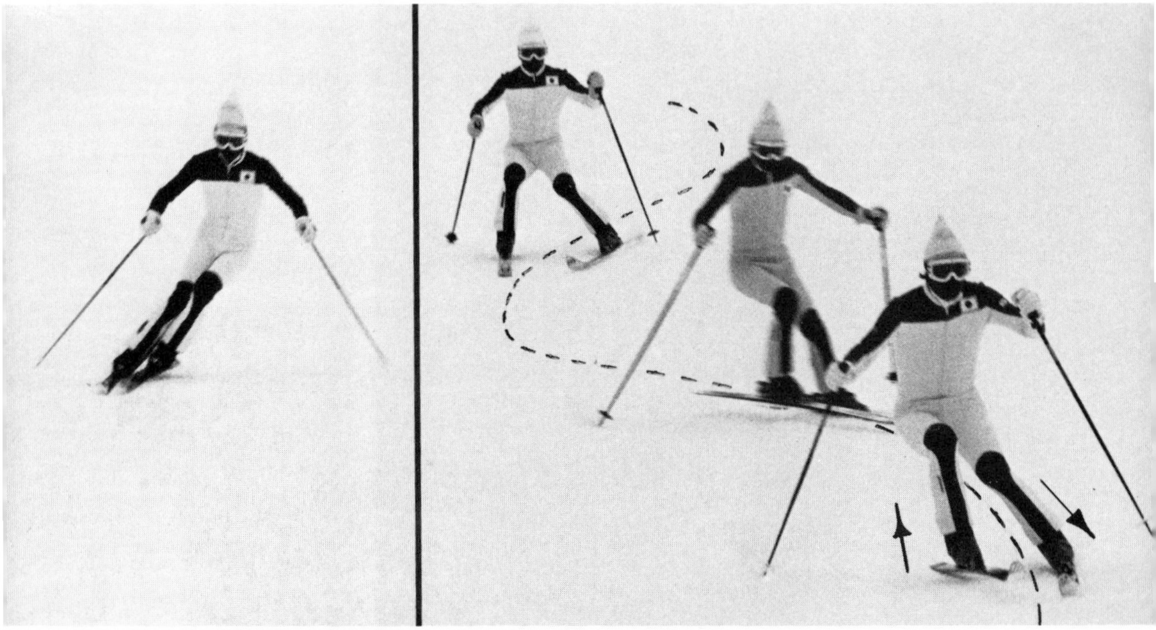

outer ski. This movement will cause your ski to become parallel and apart.

Parallels Never Meet

The single most inhibiting factor for many people when they ski is that they bring their feet and skis too close together. This makes if difficult to find the inside edge of the skis, almost impossible to press or push out against the outer ski without 'stemming' first and impossible to create appropriate 'leg lean-in' in order to steer the turns effectively.

A definition of 'parallel': lines, equidistant from each other, that *never* meet. Railway lines are parallel but they are not together.

Your feet and skis will eventually come very close together, but only when you make rhythmical, continuously linked turns at quite high speeds. So until you have achieved this level of low and dynamic balance, keep your skis apart and remember that *parallel skis never meet*.

8. Ski close to the flow line, down the 'neck' of the funnel, and you are now linking basic parallel turns. If you have difficulty in turning your inner leg you might want to 'step outside' the funnel for an hour or so and practise this particular movement. Ploughing and then steering the inner leg parallel will cause you to skid and you should enjoy this sensation. The

Fig 67 (left) Japanese demonstrators at Sexton Interski 1983 illustrate 'pedalling'. The inner leg is bent as the outer leg is extended. This identifies the tip of the inner ski in preparation for the next modification to the ploughing. Note how the hip angle remains closed throughout the extension of the outer leg. Note also the comparison of movements and shapes between the ploughers on the right and the skier showing more refined advanced movements on the left.

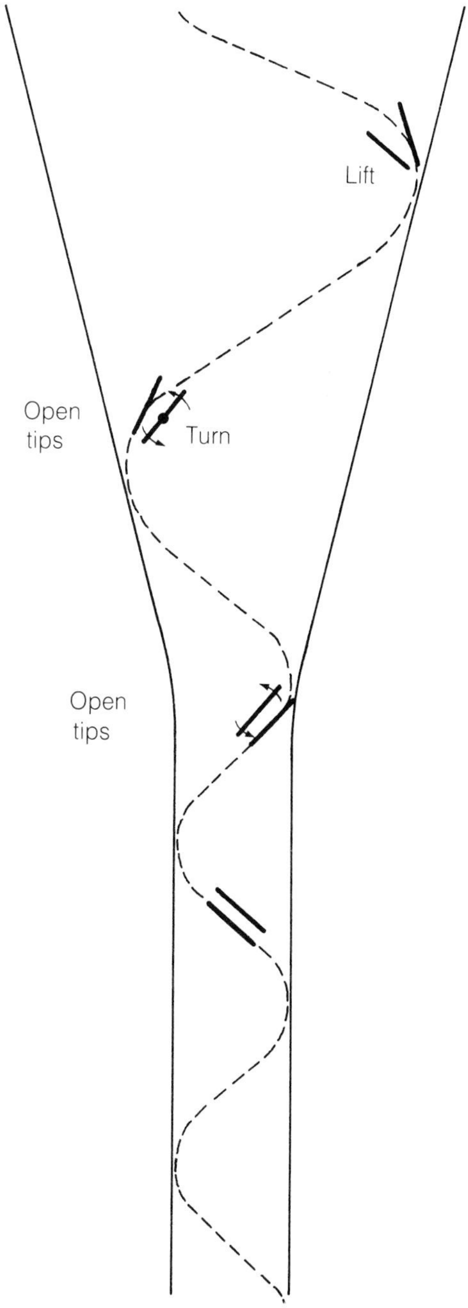

Fig 68 As you identify the tip of the inner ski, turn your leg to move the tip away from the outer ski.

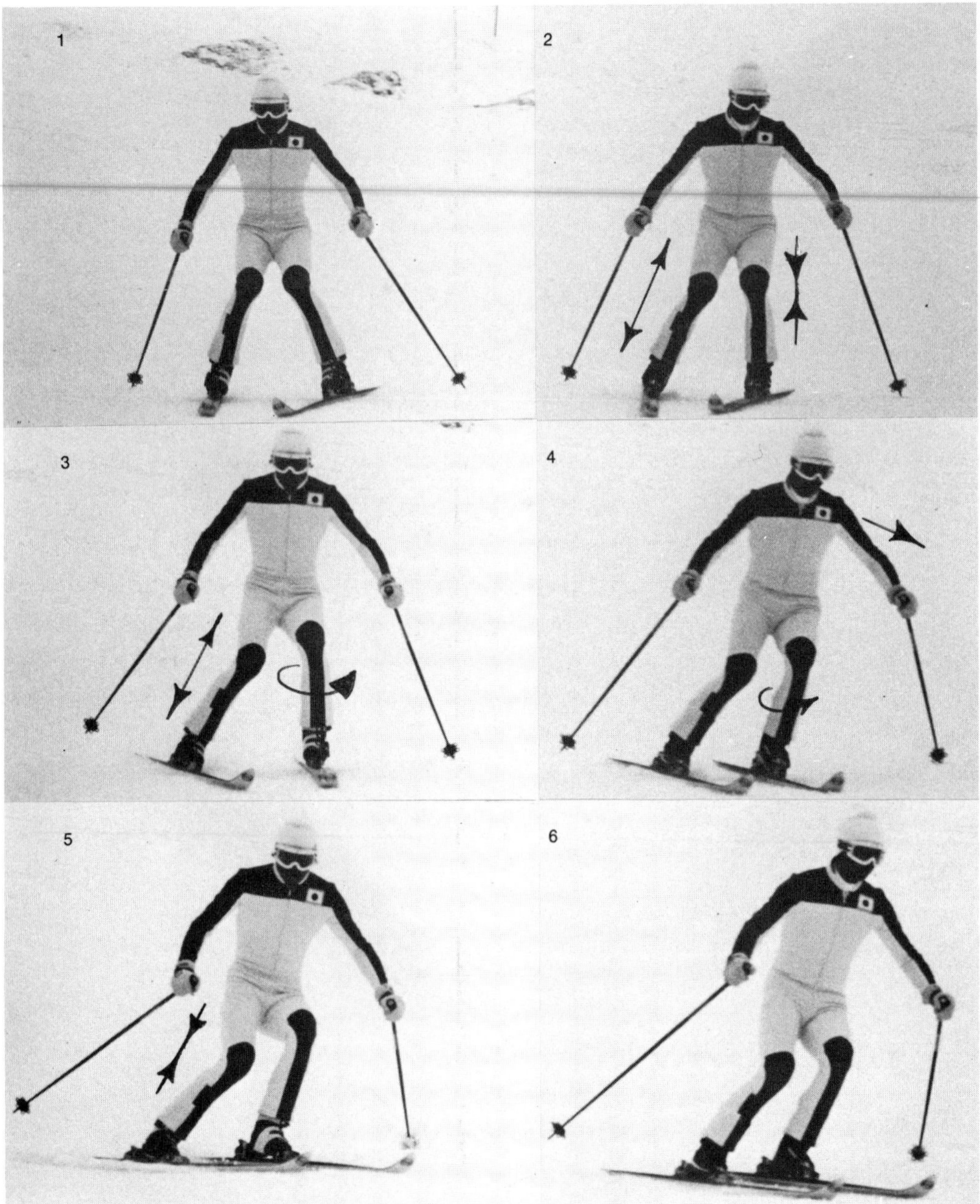

Fig 69 If you have difficulty in turning your inner leg whilst skiing in the funnel, then practise this part on its own. This exercise is called a plough swing. 1. Plough with reasonable speed. 2. Keep hip angle closed by bringing shoulders forward and down as you bend inner leg. 3. Turn inner leg and ski, ensuring that you move the tip of that ski away from the outer ski. 4. Keep your skis and legs apart and ski sideways and forwards with your skis parallel. 5. As you skid bend your legs slightly and allow your weight to flow against your outer ski. 6. Practise plough swings to both sides – with reasonable speed – before returning to the funnel.

Fig 70 A variation of the plough swing is a parallel swing to the hill. This is a steered version of a simple skid to a halt. 1. Descend with reasonable speed and stand quite erect on the heel of your inner ski. 2. Bring your shoulders forward and down by flexing at the hips and as you do so press down onto the ball of the lower/outer foot. 3. Flex knees and ankles as well as hips. 4. Maintain pressure against the ball and instep of your outer foot, steering your ski against its inner edge. Note: this voluntary movement of your body mass at an angle to the motion of your skis reinforces the tendency to skid as you flex and turn your legs to steer the skis. This movement enables the design of the ski to be fully exploited.

technique is called *plough swing*. Remember to use the design of the ski to help you to steer.

9. If you take your newly acquired movements, your linked basic parallels, onto steeper terrain you may find that the flow is too much and you run out of control. If so, you need to rhythmically introduce more resistance into the pattern of your movements. This is done by turning both your skis quickly across the line of motion and then resisting your flow with a sharp push into the snow. This action is called *checking*. When you have introduced this check – this quick and sudden resistance – into your rhythmically linked parallels you are doing *short swings*.

Short Swings *(Fig 71)*

To make the movements as easy as possible ensure that you work your ankles well. Flex and extend, turning your feet and skis whilst they are just off the ground – whilst they are unweighted. To aid the timing, and to some degree the turning forces, use a firm, short, sharp jab of your ski stick to trigger your ankle and leg extension. Feel for the rhythm: check – jab – hop – check – jab – hop. Using short swings you will be able to bring your flow back under control and so descend safely down steeper, narrowish slopes.

Always be aware of this interplay between flow and resistance, and use your awareness to keep both in delicate balance. Aim for maximum flow but use selective resistance to direct your flow. This will give you the satisfaction of control and the exhilaration of gravity powered motion – the next best thing to flight.

Fig 71 Add powerful rhythm to your movement patterns as you emerge from the neck of the funnel and you are ready to link your ability to flow and resist, in sequence, in short swings.

Fig 72 Adapt your movements to the motion and the timing of other skiers. Try formation skiing, either in pairs or small groups. When you attempt this in groups, the secret of good synchronisation is for everyone to take their timing from the front skier only.

Variations *(Figs 72 & 73)*

You are now a skilful skier. To improve your skill you must continually set yourself different tasks to solve. Develop versatility in your movements and motion, and adapt your movements to the motion which arises in different terrain and different snow conditions. Adaptability is the corner-stone for all future progress. In the meantime, you should practise all the activities in this chapter and relate the movements you make to the ideas in the other chapters. In addition, you should ski down the funnel – from beginning to end – every time you go out onto the slopes. Do it as a warm up, as a refresher and as a reminder of the need to set yourself tasks as well as techniques to practise. Do it with a variety of body shapes: ski the funnel 'standing' quite tall; ski the

Fig 73 Exploit your local dry ski centre and take part in club races which are a lot of fun. Racing will improve your accuracy and your adaptability, and encourage good independent leg action. This is shown here by Robert Zoller, 1985 World Championship bronze medallist, racing at Gloucester in the Schools Abroad All England Championships.

funnel from top to bottom in a low crouch; ski it fast in a low crouch and you will feel the need to work on your fitness preparation in order that you can develop your skiing to higher speeds or into off *piste* skiing or racing.

One final piece of advice before we leave the syllabus. Some ski schools advertise that a certain technique will enable you to ski in all conditions on all occasions without any need to change your technique. This is simply propaganda and a foolish notion which misses the point of skill in skiing. Skill is all about adaptability and versatility – coping with differing situations in effective ways, but always coping. Skill is about solving tasks efficiently and with mechanically sound movements, and skill involves learning. Thus, skill in skiing means learning to solve new tasks and by doing so improving. Trying to learn new and different techniques will be traumatic. Instead, modify what you can do, only slightly, to solve new tasks and you will become better, more skilful without really noticing the effort – and that is a characteristic of skill as well.

5 The Ski-way Code

In the early days of motoring a man with a red flag walked before the motor vehicle to warn other road users of the approaching car. Such devices have never been adopted for skiers, even though many early skiers did carry small bells on their ski sticks which could serve to warn of their approach when descending in the fog, mist or falling snow. An idea no doubt inspired by the cowbells which enable the Alpine herdsmen to find their wandering animals among the high pastures and hills. Finding modern skiers on the snow-covered alpine pastures is never a problem. Indeed the major task is often avoiding the other skiers who are using the same pathways and snow-fields, but each travelling their own individual routes.

The Highway Code has evolved as a guide to road users to enable safer and more enjoyable use of the country's roads by drivers, cyclists and pedestrians alike. A similar code of conduct for users of ski *pistes*, *Abfahrten* or skiers' runs (as they are called) has been evolved by the International Ski Federation – the FIS. The Highway Code recommends the conduct of road users, but is not itself enforceable by law. The law places the responsibility for safe and courteous behaviour firmly with the individual driver. The ski-way code, the 'rules' for the conduct of skiers, is based upon the same principle, that each individual skier is responsible for his own behaviour.

The ski-way code indicates desirable behaviour and forms the basis on which all skiers may anticipate the behaviour of others. Safe and enjoyable behaviour on busy ski slopes occurs because all the individual skiers maintain a balance between freedom to ski wherever and whenever they wish and the responsibility to do so in control and according to an agreed code of conduct. This enables every skier to most readily anticipate and so predict the actions and movements of other skiers.

The ski-way code is the internationally agreed set of rules for all responsible and keen skiers irrespective of ability, and you should be familiar with them in theory and in practice. Any skier who does not observe these rules and so behaves irresponsibly on the ski slopes lays himself open to liabilities in the case of any accident or incident in which he may be involved. The ski-way code is based upon the premiss that skiing, as with all other sports, has a risk element and certain civil and penal responsibilities.

I recommend that you familiarise yourself with the following rules before you go to the slopes and then observe them in practice. They apply equally to dry ski slopes and to mountain *pistes*.

Rule 1: Respect of Others

A skier must behave in such a way that he/she does not endanger or prejudice others. The FIS comments that this and the other rules apply to *all* skiers. The participants in competitions are, of course, bound to follow the additional specific national or international rules of the competition itself. 'The integrity of the human being stands over and above all sports results.' Even when you are in a ski class

Fig 74 The ski-way code is now published in most ski resorts.

Fig 75 Nic Fellows, who began skiing on a dry ski slope in Tetford.

these rules apply to you, your class mates and your instructor. Ski instructors must respect the rules and should teach them to their pupils and see that they are followed. If yours does not do this, then you must use your own initiative to learn and abide by the ski-way code.

Rule 2: Control of Speed and Skiing

A skier must adapt his speed and way of skiing to his personal ability and to the prevailing conditions of snow, terrain and weather. It is normal for skiers to travel quickly on 'fast', red or black, runs, and slowly on easy runs, green and blue, which are generally used by beginners. These factors must be borne in mind by skiers travelling slowly on fast runs and by better skiers travelling quickly on easy *pistes* and slopes. Whether you are a beginner or an experienced skier you must ski slowly in narrow passages and with extra care at the end of runs and near ski lifts. You should always be able to stop, make a turn or other controlling manoeuvre on the terrain within your vision.

Rule 3: Control of Direction

A skier coming from above, whose dominant position allows him a choice of pathway, must take a direction which assures the safety of the skiers below. Skiing is a 'free' activity where everyone should go as they please providing they respect the rights of other skiers to do the same and always ski 'in control'. The FIS remain very much opposed to the establishment of regulatory 'rules of the road', such as passing on the left or below others. Every skier must decide for himself how to handle the immediate situation. A normally careful and conscientious skier should be aware of what happens

Fig 76 Dennis Edwards, British men's slalom champion 1983, in training.

not only in front and below him, but also on both sides during the descent. Whilst the skier above must give way to the skier below, and therefore the lower or slower skier could be said to have 'right of way', it is incumbent upon you as a slower and lower skier to behave in a predictable manner and with due respect for the skiers approaching from above, who need to be able to predict your motion and your actions if they are to give you a safe and clear passage.

Rule 4: Overtaking

It is permitted to overtake another skier going downhill or uphill to the right or to the left, but when doing so you must always leave a wide enough margin for the overtaken skier to make or complete his turns. This rule

Fig 77 When you stop, do so in a compact group, in a prominent position at the edge of the piste. Look up and down before setting off again.

indicates that when overtaking you must not cause any difficulties for the skier being overtaken, whether he is moving or stationary at the time.

Rule 5: Crossing the Piste

A skier wishing to enter and cross a ski run must look up and down to ensure he/she can do so without endangering himself and others . . . The same applies when starting after a stop on the ski run. This rule is self explanatory; nevertheless it is quite amazing how often skiers do fail to look over their shoulder before 'pulling out' onto the slopes. Remember, give the skiers above you time to see you and avoid you when you move out into the main flow line.

Rule 6: Stopping

Avoid stopping on the ski run unless it is absolutely necessary. Never stop in constricted areas or places with poor visibility. In case of a fall, move to the side as soon as possible. If you do need to stop, then stop at the edge of the *piste*. In some countries it is considered unlawful to stop in dangerous places, such as narrow passages, inside edges of bends, out of sight, over the 'lip' of a convex slope or at the junction of two or more ski runs.

Rule 7: Climbing

A climbing skier or pedestrian must keep to the edge of the piste. In bad visibility keep off the piste completely.

Rule 8: Respect for Signals

Skiers must obey the signs. You should respect all signs which indicate if ski runs are open or closed. Signs which indicate danger points and sections of a run as closed are imperative and *must* be respected. Never ski into soft snow beyond boundary fences or past signs which indicate avalanche danger or other mountain hazards. Respect all advisory signs and always co-operate with lift company staff and members of the ski patrol.

Pistes or ski runs are marked in green, blue, red and black indicating the degree of difficulty which you will meet in one or more parts of the run ahead of you. A red run may look easy at its starting point but it will be difficult in parts so respect the *piste* markers and consult your map of the ski area before setting off down unfamiliar slopes. Choose your ski runs with care. A slow skier using a steepish run must be aware of the faster skiers approaching and always move in a visible and predictable manner. If, as a faster skier, you wish to descend an easy run, be aware that speeding past less able skiers may be very offputting to them, and remember Rule 4.

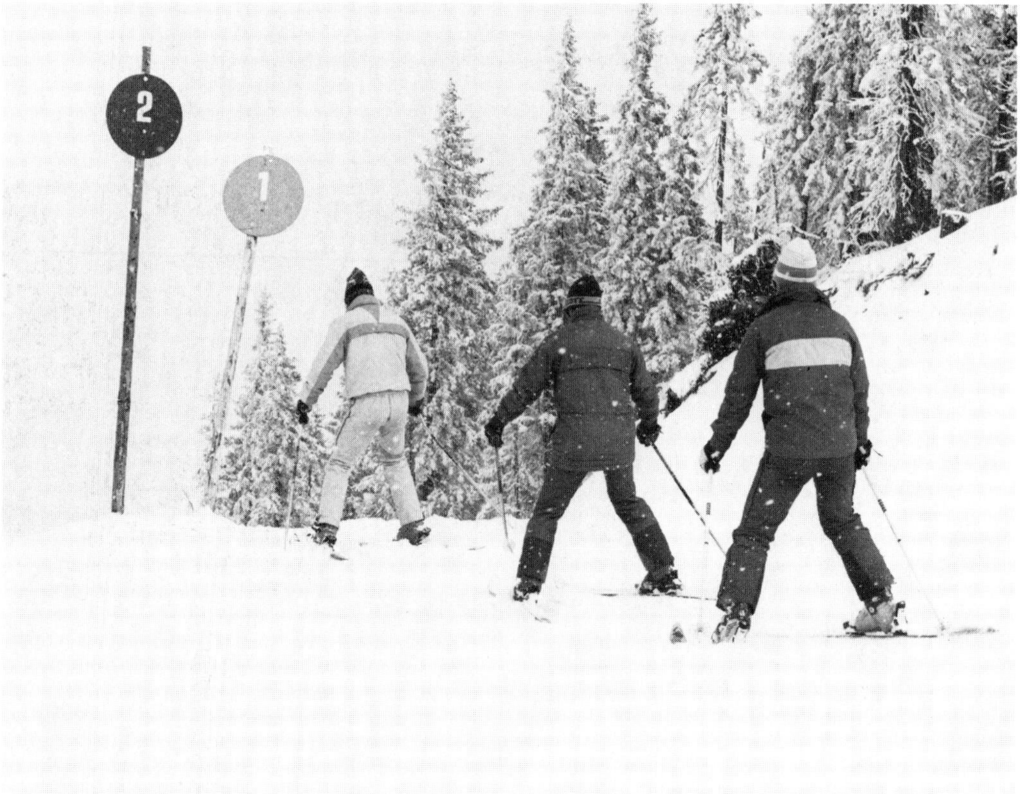

Fig 78 Pistes are marked by number and by colour which indicates the degree of difficulty you may meet in one or more parts of the run down.

AKUTE LAWINENGEFAHR
ACUTE DANGER OF AVALANCHES
Très grave danger d' avalanches!
Bei Aufleuchten der Blinkleuchte akute Lawinengefahr abseits der geöffneten und markierten Schiabfahrten
When flashing light is on, there is acute danger of avalanches off the open and marked ski-runs.
Lorseque les clignotaires s' allument très grave risque d' avalanches n' utiliser que les descentes de ski libres et marquées.

Fig 79 Obey all the signs, both on the piste and at the lift stations.

Achtung
Attention
Attenzione
Hier verlassen Sie das kontrollierte Ski-Gebiet
Ici vous quittez la zone de ski contrôlée
Qui lasciate la zona scilistica controllata
Here you are leaving the controlled skiing-region
Lawinengefahr
Danger d avalanches
Pericolo di valanghe
Danger of avalanches

Fig 80 Disobeying signs puts you at great risk. It also endangers others.

Fig 81 You may have skied on this run yesterday. If it is closed today – obey the signs.

Fig 82 Even small avalanches can kill or cripple. These skiers were fortunate to survive.

Rule 9: Conduct at Accidents

At an accident, everybody is duty bound to assist. It may be that your help is not needed if the fallen skier is part of a group. On the other hand an injured skier alone on a mountainside could quite easily die if left unattended and is missed by the ski patrol at the end of the day. In some countries it is an offence to 'desert an accident' on the roads and the same code is applied on the *pistes*.

Rule 10: Identification

Witnesses must establish their identity. If a dossier is required then the report of witnesses can be of great importance when the police or medical services try to determine possible liabilities in the cause of justice. If you see an accident clearly it is your duty to be available as a witness if required. This particular rule is not an easy one to work to if you are on holiday in a foreign land and you do not speak the language. Nevertheless you should be aware that it is a law of the land in most central European countries.

Additional Rules (Fig 84)

Modern ski equipment is designed to release in case of a fall. A runaway ski can be a lethal weapon. To prevent danger to others below you and to prevent you from losing a runaway ski or having to walk a long way to retrieve one, you should always use skis with integral ski brakes. If you intend to ski off *piste* in deep snow you should also use retaining straps for your own convenience. On the *piste* you want to be separated from your ski in a fall so that it does not flail and cut you. In deep snow however, without a retaining strap you might not find your ski unless it is attached to you in some way after it has released.

Fig 83 If you are first on the scene of an accident, stay calm and assess the situation. 1. Is the injured person breathing, bleeding, moving? 2. Delegate others to assist and take action to aid injured skier. 3. Group people together. 4. Cross skis in snow about 10 to 15 metres uphill. 5. Comfort injured skier. 6. Reassess. 7. If injured skier needs help–do not move–but send two or more good skiers for help to SOS or lift station, with details of accident, i.e. where, piste map, pylons, etc. 8. Remain calm, give comfort and keep injured person warm.

Fig 84 Use ski brakes on the piste, but if you lose a ski in deep snow in poor visibility you may spend hours looking for it without a retaining strap.

All of these rules apply when you are in a ski class as well as when you are free skiing. When you are in a class or skiing group you should observe Rules 3 and 4 particularly closely when you ski down to rejoin your group. Always give the group a wide berth and join your group at its lower edge. Never try to ski close to the group and stop at the top – if you trip or slide at the last minute the ensuing skittles can cause damage to your group members as well as yourself.

Acceptance of the ski-way code will increase your respect for others and also theirs for you. Follow the code and appreciate the freedom that it gives you to safely and responsibly enjoy the slopes and mountains.

6 Fitness

At the beginning of this century when Englishmen took to the Alps on skis there were no lifts to carry them up the snow fields, and the hardest part of the day, in physical terms, was climbing uphill rather than skiing down. Most of these skiers were at home in the mountains and able to move among them with ease. Package tours and ski lifts have enabled many millions more people to go skiing in recent years, but they also permit us to walk out of a city centre one morning and be at the top of a mountain in the afternoon. Many, perhaps too many, of us arrive in the mountains inadequately prepared to get the most out of our skiing. This is especially likely if you are a beginner, but even if you are a committed recreational skier or competitor you should consider your fitness to be a major factor in your enjoyment, safety and success.

What is Fitness? *(Figs 85 to 87)*

In general conversation fitness conjures up images of exercises, health foods and jogging and relates to improved health and the ability to keep going when others have tired. In general terms this is reasonable and shows how important it is for our bodies to be functioning properly if we are going to do our best at whatever it is we are doing. Fitness therefore can be considered from two points of view – the short term and the long term. But first, consider a definition that you can work from. 'The round peg *fits* into the round hole; the square peg will not *fit*.'

Fitness is the appropriate 'shape' or condition. Being fit means being in a suitable condition or ready for something. This definition serves to emphasise the two most important aspects of fitness. Firstly it is a prerequisite; it must be established *before* the activity takes place. Secondly it is *specific*, i.e. specific to a particular sport or activity.

Many sportsmen, competitive skiers and holidaymakers fail to achieve their potential or enjoy the sport as much as they could because of inadequate preparation. Many people believe that 'doing it' gets you fit. This is, of course, true to a very limited degree – trying to push a square peg into a round hole will eventually wear the corners off and it will fit – sort of – eventually. If you are a beginner on holiday you do not have time, and anyway 'rubbing the corners off' can mean sore feet and aching muscles. *Prior* preparation is important.

The requirements of every sport are different. The marathon runner or jogger does not need the strength in the shoulder girdle that a gymnast does. As a skier you will need to prepare your body so that it will *fit* into ski techniques easily and an emphasis on leg and abdominal preparation is appropriate if you are to control yourself and your skis (and boots) once gravity has taken you under her wing.

It is not only the movements or techniques of skiing which are specific but the environment in which you do them is also different from 'normal'. The environment ranges from high altitude and

Fig 85 Nowadays it is the exception rather than the rule to see skiers walking uphill.

low temperatures to hot discothèques late in the evening if you are a keen holidaymaker as well as a keen skier. There comes a time however when you will have to choose – skiing or dancing. Your fitness will delay this decision but eventually, in order to ski as well as you are able, as safely as possible and with as much satisfaction and success as you wish for, you must prepare yourself beforehand so that you arrive in a suitable condition to ski; so that you arrive *fit* to ski.

Benefits of Fitness
(*Figs 88 to 90*)

The most obvious benefit of fitness is that it will enable you to ski longer each day; in simple terms, to get more skiing for your money. Value for money is not only measured in terms of time spent skiing. The *quality* of your skiing is important, probably more important in satisfaction terms than the amount of skiing you do.

Fig 86 When a racer corners at speed he must be capable of withstanding the centrifugal effect of his inertia which may be up to three times his body weight–on one leg! Pirmin Zurbriggen, double World Champion, could not even hope to drive off his outer ski during this Giant Slalom unless he had developed his leg power beforehand.

Fig 87 The environment for skiing can embrace hot discos and hotels at high altitudes and very low temperatures.

Fitness

Fitness improves the quality of your skill as a skier. In order that techniques can be performed efficiently, effectively and with a minimum of effort – the characteristics of a skilful performance – it is necessary that the muscles which control your movements are capable of doing the work involved in the specific techniques. If these muscles are too weak or if your suppleness is insufficient to allow your body to assume the correct shapes and movement patterns then other muscles will be called in to assist. This will result in the techniques being learned and performed inadequately.

The effect of repeating incorrect or inefficient movement patterns will be to cause you to develop problems in your skiing which will hinder your progress. The

Fig 88 Fitness is a prerequisite for the development of skill.

Fig 89 Inadequate fitness will mean that quality of skiing will deteriorate rapidly during the day. It may mean that anxiety or fatigue prevents the learner from ever acquiring efficient movements in the first place.

saying 'if at first you don't succeed, try, try, try again' is not very good advice. It should be 'if at first you don't succeed, give up' or at least 'give up that movement and try a different one'. Remember practice makes perfect but only if you are doing it right! The only way to prevent the practice of undesirable movements becoming undesirable habits is to ensure that you are in a suitable condition to do it right first time. Having appropriate strength and mobility will therefore help you to learn the correct movements. In addition, endurance will enable you to keep practising the correct movements for more repetitions thus speeding up your learning.

Fitness delays the onset of fatigue locally, in practising techniques and learning patterns of movements as well as giving you more hours for your money. Fatigue, as well as causing a diminution of quality of technique, also causes reduction in attention and quality of perception. This together with impaired technique can cause a rise in anxiety, which provokes a reduction in your level of skill, so starting a vicious circle, as well as spoiling your enjoyment and exhilaration.

Fitness will not only delay the onset of fatigue but it will allow you to recover more quickly after becoming fatigued. Fatigue delayed means a reduction in the probability of an accident. Thus fitness enhances your safety. If you should fall

Fig 90 Fitness will lessen the probability of accidents – but if you should fall, fitness will reduce the risk of injury too.

and hurt yourself, fitness will lessen the probability of serious injury. Fitness will reduce the amount and severity of the damage to joints, muscles and tendons. Fitness acquired before you go onto the ski slopes will enhance the quality of your learning, improve your safety and increase your enjoyment satisfaction and rate of progress. But how much and for how long before do you have to improve your fitness to gain these benefits?

DEVELOPING FITNESS

Short Term

This is the process which you will adopt to prepare yourself in the period immediately prior to going skiing. In order to be as fit as you can, this preparation should last at least two months and preferably longer – up to six months. In short-term development of fitness you will seek to maximise your current physical capacities in preparation for a short burst of skiing. This might be your skiing holiday or it might be one or more specific events if you are a competitor. The period you choose for the development of short-term fitness is called your period of *preparation training*.

If you are a competitor approaching national or international standards then your preparation training period will last several years and your short-term development is called *high performance competition training*. The objective of this form of training is to produce in each athlete, individually, a *peak* of physical and mental fitness together with maximum skill development that will enable him or her to achieve their best performance in competition. It can only be achieved after several years of preparation training with total commitment from the individual skier. Anything less than one hundred per cent application and effort will result in the non-realisation of full potential. This category of training requires well in excess of twenty hours per week of high quality work. It is the most sophisticated of training in both the methods used and the monitoring of personal and performance factors. This training will be done within a close continuing relationship with a coach.

High performance competition training, therefore, is a short-term training phase within a recurring long-term cyclic pattern. This long-term training cycle begins for top international athletes when they are children. To a very large degree the ultimate potential of all of us as skiers or athletes of any kind is determined partly by our genes, our inherited characteristics, but largely by the nature of our lifestyle and in particular the nature of our long-term development of fitness.

Long Term

Your best performance as a skier will be achieved when you are an adult, all other factors such as access to training and so on being equal. It takes between twenty and twenty-five years for the human body to grow into full adult maturity. What you do with your body when it is growing determines your ultimate level of attainment and is, in fact, the 'programme' which will develop your long-term fitness. The activites which you do in this period of growth and development can be classified into three parts:

1. *Foundation training.*
2. *Preparation training.*
3. *High performance competition training.*

From a committed athlete's point of view high performance competition training will appear to be the most important phase. From a committed recreational skier's point of view the preparation training phase will be what he thinks of as fitness training. From the coach's viewpoint, however, it is the *foundation training* phase which, as its name suggests, is the vital base on which future development depends.

Foundation Training (Figs 92 to 95)

In the main, foundation training is concerned with the development of the functional qualities of agility, balance, co-ordination and confidence. The emphasis is on play within a variety of activities. The key factors in sound foundation training are variety and fun with attention to agility, balance, co-ordination, posture, confidence and mobility as themes within the various activities. These activities are related to the needs of a child rather than the needs of any specific sport and its narrow technical disciplines. Foundation training mostly occurs outside the control of the coach. It is a responsibility of primary and lower secondary education and is augmented by the normal play and games of children and youths in family and peer group recreation.

Fig 91 The long-term training cycles begin for top athletes when they are children. Our genes and our lifestyle determine our potential in any field, but especially in skiing where balance, co-ordination, agility and courage are needed in good measures.

Ideal foundation training ensures that children and youths participate in activities which will enhance the normal growth and development of their bodies. All aspects of our growth and development do not occur at the same rate nor at the same time and it is important that any planned activity relates to the anatomical, physiological and psychological development of each individual. For example, in the early years of life *neural* development occurs at a faster rate than other aspects and so activities encouraging co-ordination, elementary balance, language and relationships are important. In the middle and late childhood the body's systems, e.g. the cardio-respiratory or vascular systems, may be enhanced by increasing endurance as a factor in play. On the other hand, the growth of bones and muscles does not occur at an even rate and it is vital that these are not subjected to heavy loading until after the completion of the pubertal growth spurts. Skeletal development is not simply an increase in height and weight. Changes also occur in the nature and structure of the bones themselves. Growing bones are preformed of cartilage which is weaker than bone.

During maturation ossification takes place as the cartilage is replaced with bone tissue. Skeletal ossification is not complete until approximately twenty-five years of age.

It is important for coaches and all skiers taking responsibility for their own training to be aware that growing bones are not only more pliable than mature ones, but they are not as strong and cannot endure heavy loads. Medical research has shown that sub-maximal loading stimulates length growth and may therefore be encouraged, whilst excessive loading inhibits growth. It is advisable to err on the side of caution and use only body weight in exercising until late adolescence.

It is worth noting also that normal growth patterns mean that children are generally more supple, have greater joint mobility, in their pre-pubescent years than in later adolescence. Good mobility is an important aspect of fitness for skiing and is harder to regain in adulthood than it is to maintain from childhood. It is never too late to start mobility – 'stretching' – exercises, but they are important in the years of early adolescence when strength training is undesirable and growth spurts often cause temporary reductions in agility and co-ordination, giving impressions of awkwardness, and inconsistency in

Fig 92 Ideal foundation training begins very early in life, but even for teenagers co-ordination and balance can still be enhanced.

Fig 93 Children's games can be made ski specific and used to enrich a fitness training programme.

Fig 94 Children are generally more supple than adults – 'Thank goodness!' says this youngster trying to get to grips with his new long and heavy feet.

technical performances. At such times it is important to *limit* the introduction of new movements and instead *consolidate* movement patterns that have already been learned. Understanding, patience and wisdom by coaches, by skiers themselves and by their parents is essential for sound development through what is for many young people a very trying and difficult period.

It is possible that many British children may not be introduced to skiing until very late in their foundation training phase. Indeed it may already be complete in the formal educational sphere when skiing is taken up. It is very important to realise that these 'late starters' can still reach the same level of technical attainment as those who were introduced to skiing at an earlier age. It is even possible that their ultimate attainment may in some cases be higher, providing of course that their foundation training was thorough in every other respect. For children who have been able to take part in skiing since early childhood, early maturation may lead to a relatively high standard of performance by virtue of some children's temporary physical superiority. Some such early developers are often caught and overtaken by late developers whose sound foundations enable them to compensate for lack of specific skiing experience. Thus it is futile to place too much importance on the successes or failures of the young.

From the preceding part of this chapter you have seen that your eventual level of fitness for skiing will depend upon your long-term development or foundation training and your short-term development or preparation training. When planning your preparation training, therefore, you should take into account the extent and variety of your own foundation training.

Fig 95 During adolescence it is vital that skiers, parents and coaches encourage good posture and sound basic technique, and limit the introduction of new movements until the child is strong enough to benefit from them and exploit them fully.

You can never completely recapture any experiences which were missed as a child, but you can still maintain a variety in physical activities which will reduce your weaknesses, whilst your specific preparation training will build in those areas and enhance your strengths.

Preparation Training (Fig 96)

The objective of preparation training is to develop your condition, with exercises and activities which will relate specifically to skiing. A sound preparation training programme should be tailored to your individual needs and you should seek personal advice from an expert coach if

Fig 96 Any preparation training programme should include other sports and activities which demand agility, co-ordination and quick leg work.

possible. If you cannot obtain such help then you should include in your programme the following objectives:

1. Maintain good health.
2. Improve your co-ordination and agility by participation in other games and activities. This is particularly important for younger skiers who should still devote at least fifty per cent of their recreation to sports other than skiing.
3. Improve your stamina, mobility, posture and muscular efficiency (that is muscular endurance, power and strength).

Health

It is not unusual in general conversation for fitness to be confused with health. In a sporting context it is not reasonable to interchange the two words when referring to physical condition. There is a significant difference between a healthy skier and a fit skier. It is possible for you to be healthy but yet unfit. It is *not* possible for you to be fit but unhealthy. Health must be regarded as a precondition for fitness just as fitness is a prerequisite to participation and performance.

Poor health and lack of fitness must be differentiated in order to understand the recommended courses of action in both cases. Ill health refers to *illness*, that is infection or disease, and should be treated by a doctor. Lack of fitness may be due to lack of appropriate physical work, but it may be influenced by injury. Fitness can be improved with the help of a coach, but in the case of injury a sports medical specialist should diagnose and recommend treatment which may then be followed through by physiotherapist or coach. It is possible and frequently desirable for an injured skier to continue with some aspects of training. On the other hand, it is generally undesirable for an unhealthy skier to continue training, as exercise may result in a further deterioration of health if the body is fighting a general infection or disease.

In the long term and during your skiing you can take steps to safeguard your health by attending to personal hygiene, getting plenty of rest and sleep, avoiding the harmful effects of drugs, alcohol and tobacco, and being aware of nutrition.

Nutrition

The issues of diet and weight control are related to fitness, but in general terms a balanced diet will satisfy your nutritional needs. A balanced diet is balanced in two ways. Firstly, the diet itself is balanced internally. That is to say your diet, your intake of food and drink, should contain appropriate proportions of protein, carbohydrate, fat, vitamins, minerals and water. In simple terms, protein is needed to build and repair body tissue (it is needed more in training than during competition); carbohydrate and fat provide energy for your activity, and vitamins, minerals and water make the body work.

Exercise causes loss of water and salts (minerals) which will seriously impair muscular efficiency. Dehydration is also accelerated by altitude and by the intake of alcohol. When skiing in the Alps, therefore, you must ensure that you drink sufficient non-alcoholic liquids (containing water) to keep your body fluid levels sound. Skiing is a high energy sport and requires a reasonable intake of carbohydrates during training and competition. Carbohydrate supplies glycogen in the muscles which is the main source of energy during exercise. You should therefore ensure that you eat plenty of carbohydrates preferably from starchy foods and foods high in fibre, which will enable your body to supply glycogen to your muscles in the most effective manner. Fresh rather than highly processed foods will also provide you with your normal requirements of minerals and vitamins.

How much of these foods should you eat? This is the other aspect of a balanced diet. The input of energy through food and water should balance the needs of your body's energy output from growth and exercise. This balance is easily controlled by monitoring your weight. If you eat too little, body weight will be lost as your body draws first on its reserves of fat and eventually even on body protein for its energy, which is needed to ski and to keep warm. If you eat too much, weight will be gained as energy is stored as fat. You should determine your prime or ideal weight and then adjust your eating and exercise to achieve it – slowly. Then you should maintain your prime weight with a balanced diet.

Weight

You probably know what your ideal weight should be, perhaps from height/weight charts on scales. If not then you can calculate it by using what is called your *body mass index*. This is calculated as follows: weight in kg ÷ (height × height in cm). This index will be a number beginning with two noughts; ignore these and read the next two digits which are your body mass index – between twenty and twenty-five is normal. For example, if my weight is 66kg and my height is 167cm, then my body mass index is 66 ÷ (167 x 167) = . (00)23665. My body mass index is therefore 23, which means that I am currently at my prime weight, with a diet where my food input and energy output through exercise are balanced. If your body mass index is outside the normal range you should adjust your food intake and your exercise output. To excel at skiing you should have a good power to mass ratio. As your training progresses you should, therefore, aim to improve your strength and power without increasing your body mass.

Serious fitness training programmes for competitive skiers need to be individually tailored to each skier. If you are a keen skier or keen to ski well but cannot find a coach to help you then you should start to improve your fitness – beginning today – with the following priorities.

Planning Your Programme

(Fig 97)

Before you start exercising work out how much time you usually have available, each day and each week, and plan your programme of exercises to fit in with home and work. Try to train with someone else, this will give you more fun and satisfaction. Nevertheless, remember to work on your own programme to improve your weaknesses and improve your fitness for skiing. Bear in mind the following principles.

1. *Progressive overload.* This means gradually and progressively increasing both the 'work load' and the time spent working.
2. *Systematic approach.* This means that you should follow a system geared to your needs which gives you realistic targets.

Plan your programme so that you alternate hard work sessions with easier ones, and ensure that you rest completely at least one day a week.

At the beginning of your programme do more stamina and mobility work, with some strength, power and endurance work along with posture exercises. As your programme progresses gradually change the proportions so that your muscular efficiency, posture and mobility receive most attention just before you go skiing. If you are a competitive skier you will ski regularly during the winter and your skiing itself will provide the main source of muscular efficiency training, which you must supplement with mobility and some strength training. Take a month of 'active rest' during May, ready to begin the training cycle again in June. At this time reassess your time available for training and adjust your programme accordingly.

Programme Content

Bear in mind your age and current level of fitness. Never stress yourself so much that you feel 'distressed' – start off by reaching mild breathlessness and always warm up

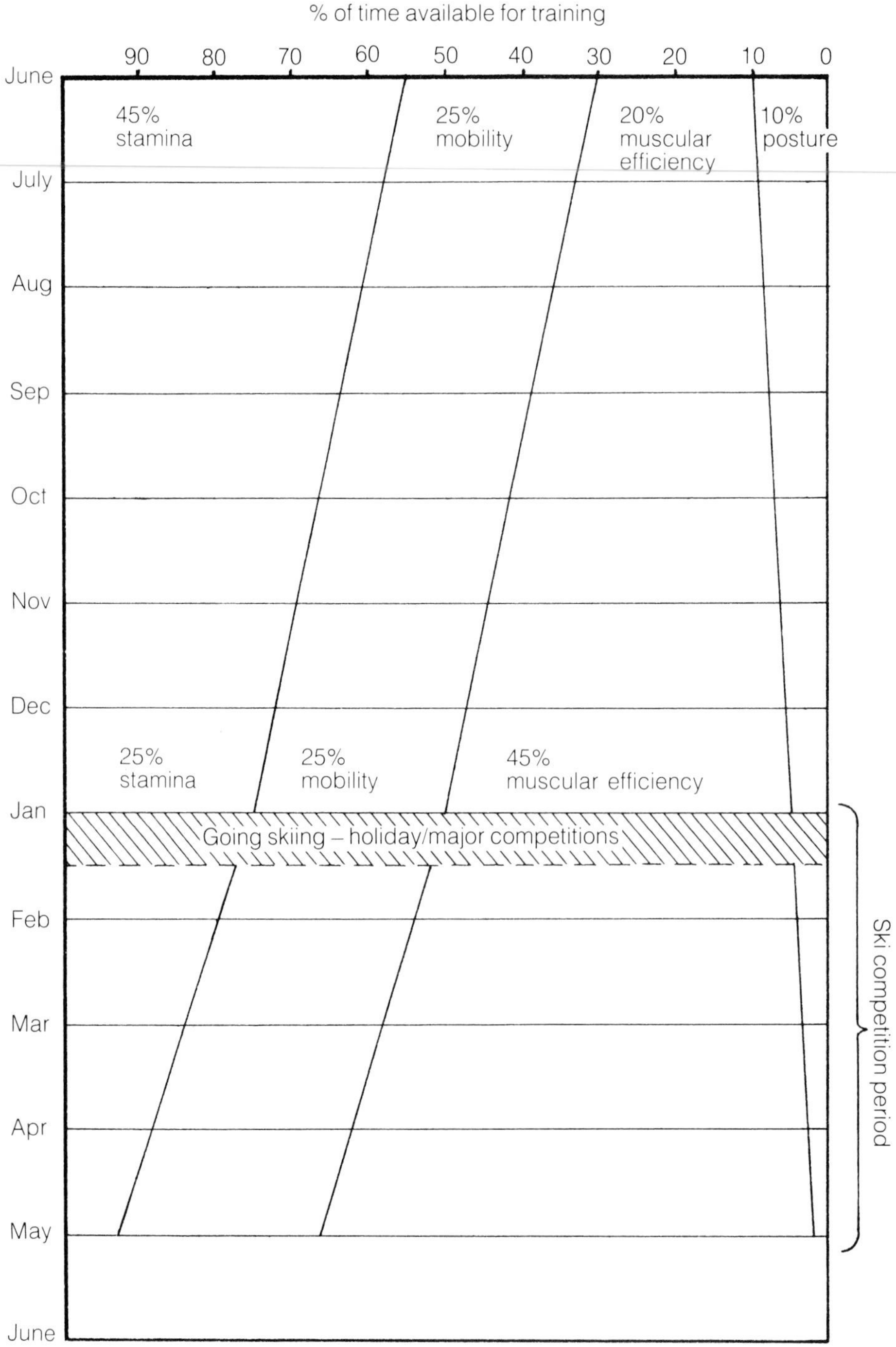

Fig 97 Annual programme showing distribution of types of training thoughout the year.

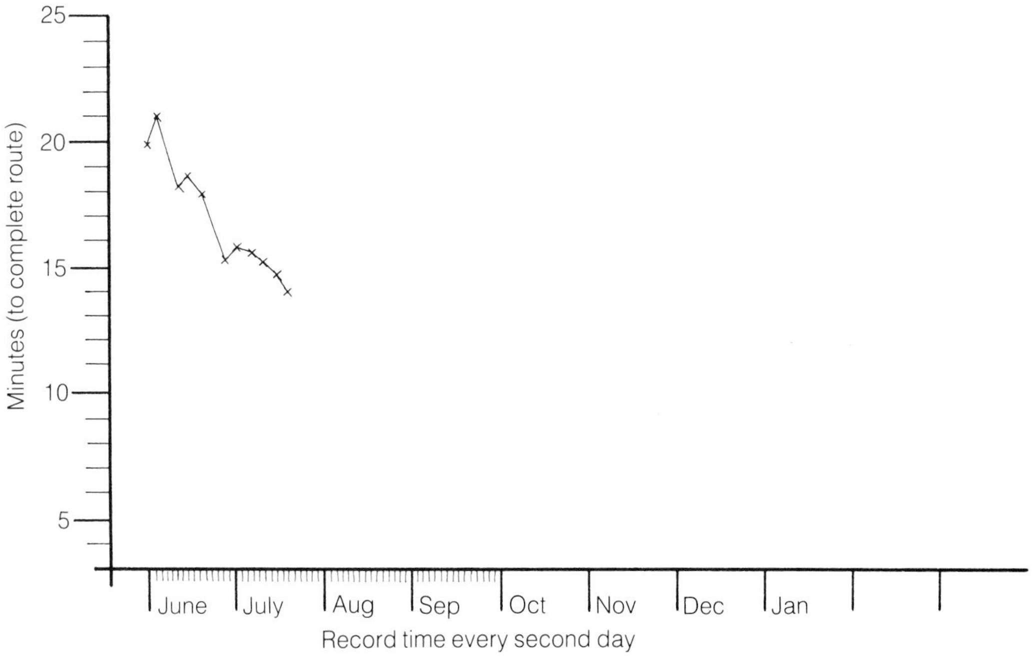

Fig 98 Feedback for your initial stamina training.

with *gentle* exercises before you begin your daily work out. Remember also that you should never use weights to increase work load unless you have either learned the correct techniques for lifting them, or you have used your own body weight first. On no account use weights other than your own body weight if you are still growing.

Warm Up

All fitness training depends upon the adaptation and growth of your body and its systems, which in turn occurs most effectively if all parts are working with appropriate nutrients and efficient transport to the muscles of these nutrients, and then from the muscles of the waste products of metabolism. Ten minutes or so of gentle but 'all over' exercise will open the blood flow system and warm up your engine. At the end of the sessions warm down gently; this helps clear the waste products and so aids recovery and offsets muscle soreness and stiffness which the waste 'metabolites' of exercise sometimes cause.

Stamina (Fig 98)

If you are not very fit this is where you start. Improve the efficiency of your heart–lung system and you will then be able to get more oxygenated blood to the parts that need it, when they need it. Cycling, swimming, skipping and jogging are all good forms of stamina training – as long as you keep your pulse rate up for about twenty minutes or more.

If you are over thirty years of age or have not done much exercise recently then *walk* briskly around a route from home about one mile to a mile and a half, and remember it. On a piece of graph paper plot time (in minutes) on the left side against dates along the bottom edge. Walk around your route and record the date and time taken to complete the route. (A stop-watch will be useful in your training programme.) Repeat this every other day and try walking and jogging, then jog and then run around your route, plotting your time each day you do it. The resulting graph will tell you how you are getting on and provide feedback which will both

Fig 99 This exercise stretches the hamstrings, inner thigh, buttocks and back muscles. It should be done to both sides and as part of a series which works around all the major muscle groups.

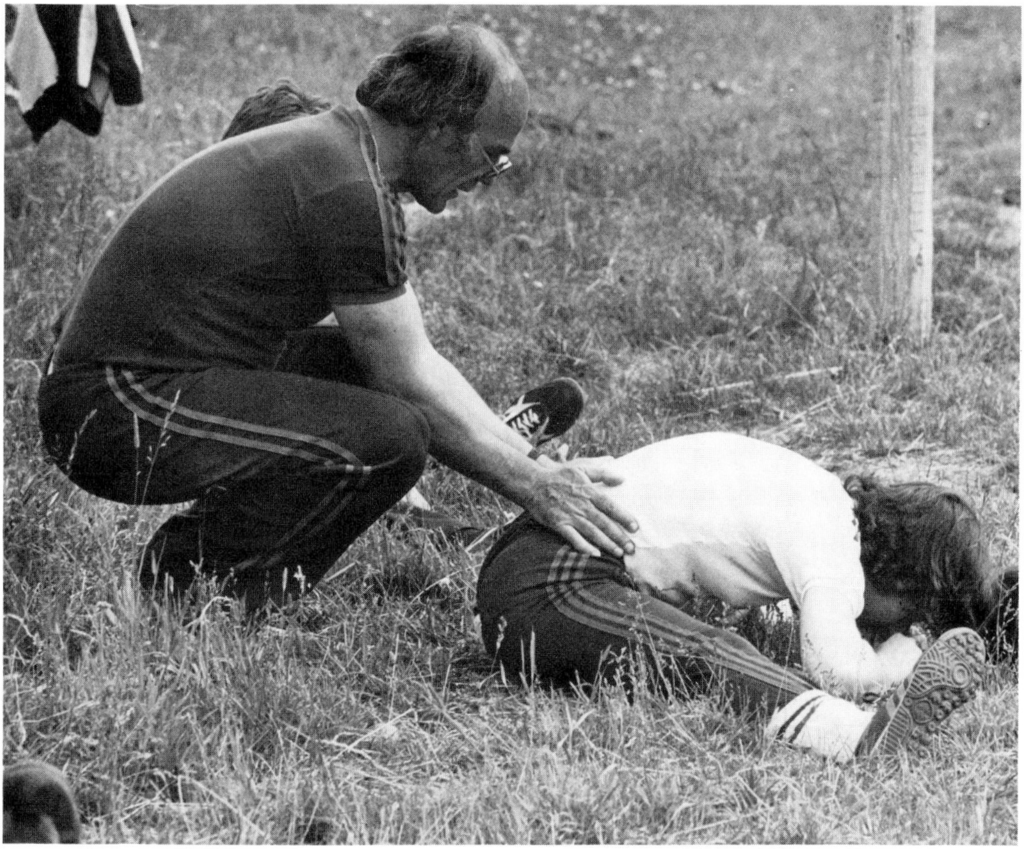

Fig 100 Warm up before stretching and then keep warm with appropriate clothing whilst stretching. Stan Palmer acts as a resistance for Sarah to push back against, before stretching a little further down. On no account should coach or partner force you to bend in this or any other exercise.

motivate and regulate your laps, especially if you pin it up on your wall at home. When your time is down to twelve minutes increase the length of your route by another half a mile and start again.

You need good training shoes for running in. 'Sorbothane' inners are good for reducing heel strike shock. At first jog on level smooth surfaces, but as you become stronger seek different surfaces – smooth grass is more pleasant to run on than paving stones.

Mobility (Figs 99 & 100)

This describes the suppleness of your limbs in movement and is achieved by stretching the muscles over and around your joints. Stretching exercises are important for two reasons; firstly to increase the range of movement in your joints, which in turn aids muscle efficiency and agility and reduces the possibility of injury during activity. Secondly to prevent the reduction of the range of movement of your limbs and joints after exercise. Working muscles hard causes them to become bulkier and shorter and therefore as you become stronger you will also become stiffer unless you do some stretching exercises.

Select several exercises and attend to mobility of your legs, hips, trunk and shoulders. There are two methods, only one of which I recommend to you. The first method is the *slow stretch* method. This method is the safest and the most effective but requires more patience on your part – not because it works more slowly, but because you do and may not feel its effect at the time.

1. Warm up.
2. Move to limit of normal movement.
3. Hold this position for 5–10 seconds.
4. During this time relax but hold the position.
5. Now stretch a little – feel some slight discomfort – and hold the position for 10 seconds or so.
6. Repeat this process three or four times for each exercise in your programme.

Fig 101 Good posture is practised from the beginning.

The second method, the *ballistic* method, involves 'bouncing' or swinging when you reach your limit of normal movement. This method can cause damage if you bouce too far and, by a subtle and sensitive protective mechanism which will try to prevent damage, this method can actually cause your muscles to shorten rather than lengthen. The ballistic or bounce method is not recommended for you in this programme.

Posture (Figs 101 & 102)

Posture is the shape of your body in relation to the movements you are asking of yourself. Posture is a predeterminant of mechanical efficiency. In skiing the legs support, propel and control the movements of your body; and the difference between good and poor skiing posture relates to the way you 'stand' against your feet and the tilt of your pelvis or the shape of your lumber spine in relation to your hips and legs.

Poor posture can be caused by all sorts of factors which include lack of awareness and attention to the problem, but in skiers poor posture is most often seen, among beginners, in females rather than males, and especially in those who frequently wear high heels which cause a shortening of the calf muscles, so restricting flexion (dorsi) of the ankles, and a hollowing of the lower back. Ski boots which do not permit ankle flexion and which may also

Fig 102 Poor posture will result in mechanically ineffective movements.

Fig 103 Immense muscular efficiency enables Marc Girardelli to remain calm despite a loss of control of his outer ski. Superb balance and co-ordination (note the extreme extension of one leg and the extreme flexion of the other) based on strength and endurance enable him to lift himself off his inner ski and on to victory in the 1985 World Cup.

have raised heels can accentuate this problem in both men and women. Posture can be improved through stretching exercises for the calf muscles, together with strengthening of the abdominal muscles. Posture is considered in Chapter 3 as an important component of dynamic balance.

Muscular Efficiency (Figs 103 & 104)

Muscular efficiency has three components: endurance, strength and power. All three aspects are closely related and training to emphasise one will have an effect on the other two. In simple terms endurance, the ability to sustain work against reasonable resistance, is achieved through repetitive work. Strength, which is the ability to create force, is achieved by working against considerable resistance. Power, which is the ability to use your strength quickly, is achieved by doing repetitions against considerable resistance with increasing speed of movements. If you are an adult competitive skier you will benefit from a tailor-made weight training programme, but if you are still growing or you are wishing to increase your muscular efficiency for recreational skiing, then circuit training is the most useful method.

Circuit Training
(Figs 105 & 106)

Circuit training is so called because you do several exercises one after the other in a circuit. This method of training will improve muscular efficiency and should initially be aimed at improving muscular endurance and power with the benefit of gains in strength. Design your circuit in the following way.

Fig 104 Sarah Lewis, Britain's best female technical skier, has achieved her current level of skill as a result of accurate application of her considerable muscular efficiency, which she uses to power her, stabilise her and keep the quality of her technique training high by delaying the onset of fatigue.

1. Draw out a diagram of your circuit with exercises for different parts of your body following each other.
2. Take your time and work your way through all the exercises, doing them well. Record how many repetitions of each exercise you can do in one minute. This is your test rate.
3. Divide your test rate by two and write this number in the training rate box.

You are now ready to begin. After a warm-up get ready for the first exercise. Start your stop-watch and work your way continuously round your circuit doing the

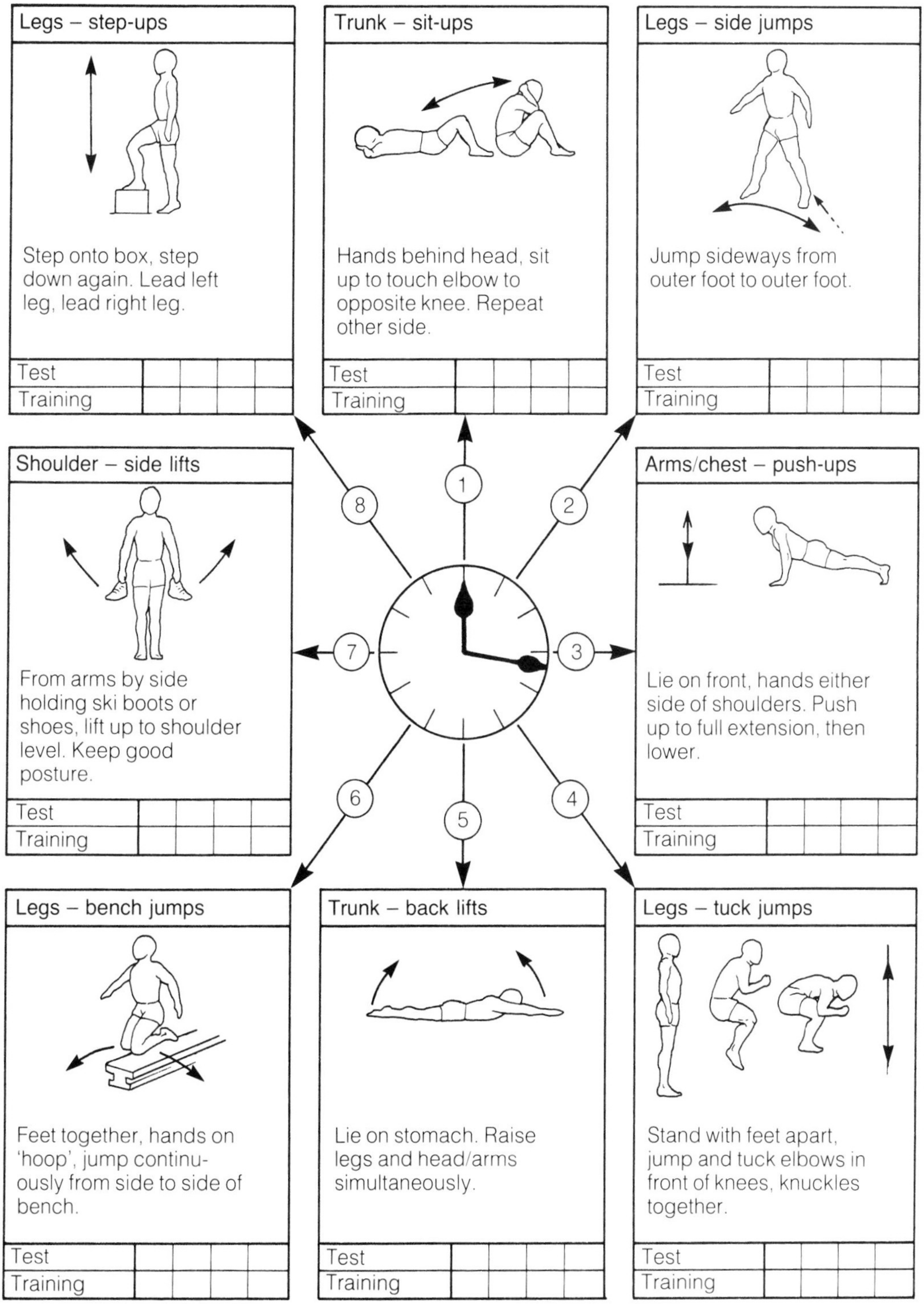
Legs – step-ups
Step onto box, step down again. Lead left leg, lead right leg.
Test
Training
Trunk – sit-ups
Hands behind head, sit up to touch elbow to opposite knee. Repeat other side.
Test
Training
Legs – side jumps
Jump sideways from outer foot to outer foot.
Test
Training
Shoulder – side lifts
From arms by side holding ski boots or shoes, lift up to shoulder level. Keep good posture.
Test
Training
1
2
3
4
5
6
7
8
Arms/chest – push-ups
Lie on front, hands either side of shoulders. Push up to full extension, then lower.
Test
Training
Legs – bench jumps
Feet together, hands on 'hoop', jump continuously from side to side of bench.
Test
Training
Trunk – back lifts
Lie on stomach. Raise legs and head/arms simultaneously.
Test
Training
Legs – tuck jumps
Stand with feet apart, jump and tuck elbows in front of knees, knuckles together.
Test
Training

Fig 105 Circuit training diagram.

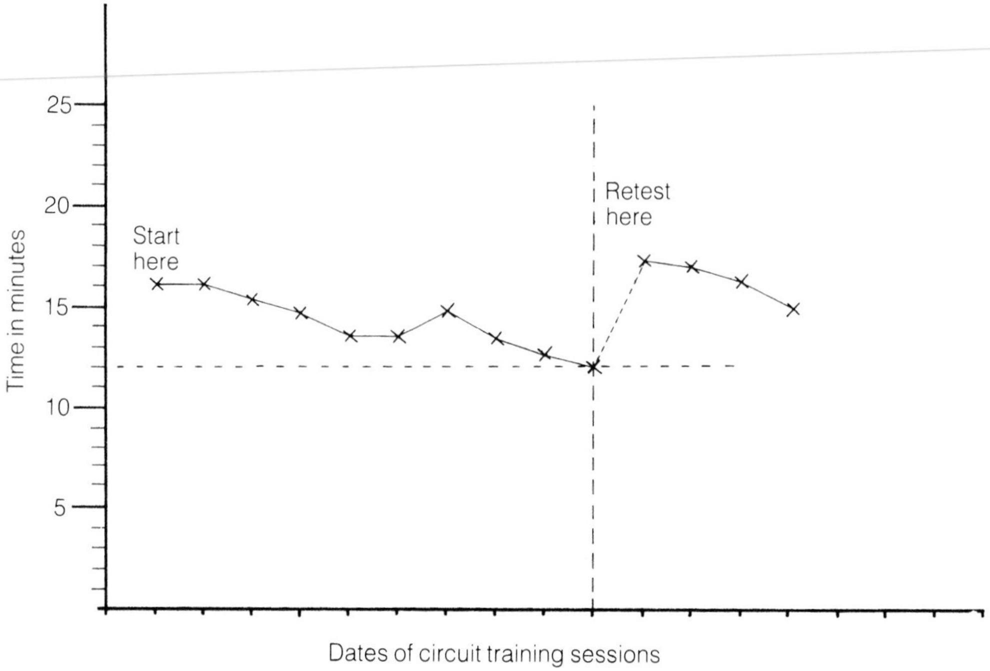

Fig 106 Circuit training feedback.

training rate number of repetitions of each exercise. Do two laps of the circuit and record your time. If you can, go on and do a third lap and record your time for all three laps. When you have completed three circuits (if possible) warm down gently and do a couple of stretching exercises to complete your training session.

At each successive circuit training session, try to complete the three laps, doing all the exercises with good form in a shorter time than at the last session. When you have reduced your time by a quarter, retest yourself to determine new test and training rates. Visual feedback from a graph will encourage you and show you how you are progressing.

Keeping Fit *(Fig 107)*

Once you have begun to plan and follow your own fitness training programme ensure that you benefit fully by avoiding injury. Always wear appropriate clothing and keep yourself warm during and after exercise. Wear strong shoes that fit well with good soles which grip when you are running and exercising. Always wear clean socks and underclothes for hygiene, but also to prevent soreness. This is especially important when you are skiing. Change and wash your ski socks every two days – each day if your feet sweat. Sweating causes salt to crystalise in the wool of your socks (never wear nylon) and these crystals can rub and cause blisters or raw skin.

Fig 107 Fit – in a suitable condition or ready for. Notice how Sarah's fitness enables her to attack her skiing so positively and confidently. Notice also that despite her speed, her movements are remarkably similar to those you learned in Chapter 4 in the second part of the funnel. Control – adaptability – small modifications – these are the secrets of success.

If you feel any pain or see swelling when you are training *stop* and seek medical advice. This is especially important if the pain is in the legs, and vital if it is in the knees of growing adolescents. Because of its mobility, its size and its position in the leverage systems during skiing, the knee is very vulnerable to twisting forces. If you experience any pain associated with either a fall or over-use of the knees in training then stop immediately and consult a doctor.

Good technique combined with good judgements about where and when to ski will enhance your overall protection and safety given by your improved fitness. To ensure that you always ski as skilfully as you are able, take a rest when you are fatigued. Fatigue, which is delayed by fitness training, will also disappear earlier, the fitter you are. So avoid pushing yourself when you are tired on the ski slopes, and look forward to another exhilarating day tomorrow, refreshed and in a suitable condition to ski to the limits of your skill.

Glossary

Angulation A movement of the body when balancing in motion. It is a flexing at the hips as the legs are rotated and skis edged to initiate a change in motion. This is also known as hip angulation. Knee angulation, a medial movement of the knee is a fine tuning movement within hip angulation.

Avalement A technique which involves forward projection of feet *and* flexion of legs to absorb *unwanted* pressure build-up between skis and snow during a turn or other manoeuvre. Literally a 'swallowing' of the excess pressure.

Ballistic Motion In skiing terms, the sensation of being carried along by your own inertia. True ballistic motion only occurs when a skier is airborne, but is often perceived when at or near the limit of control.

Coach One who coaches skiers. Usually on a long-term basis, with a regular and caring contact relationship which seeks to develop the whole performer in addition to the technical aspects of skiing.

Compression Turns *See* Wellen.

Edging A lateral tilting of the ski(s). The action causes the base or sole of the ski to be presented to the direction of motion or potential motion.

Entropy The tendency to move to the lowest energy state available.

Feedback Information arising as a consequence of an action or movements.

The Funnel The imaginary (can be constructed) shape laid out on a ski slope which is used as a target for basic ski techniques. The funnel is a *task* which, if solved, will cause the development of skill by modification and application of techniques.

The Hoop An imaginary concept which indicates where and how the hands and arms should be in relation to the skier and his ski sticks in general skiing.

Inertia The tendency of an object (mass) to remain stationary or to continue to move uniformly unless acted upon by an external force.

Kinaesthesis The kinaesthetic *perception* which links proprioception (the internal sense of shape, movement and balance) with vision and other senses to give the *perceptual* process of movement and motion awareness.

Motion The path or passage of the skier travelling on the ski slopes.

Movement The displacement of body segments in relation to each other and/or of them in relation to the skis.

Parallel Skis pointing in the same direction *and* on the same edges. Parallel skis need not be together.

Parallel Turns Parallel turns are executed when boths skis are pivoted and 'edge changed' simultaneously.

Ploughing (Snowploughing) A skier in motion ploughs when both skis are displaced at an angle to his/her flow line and skid slightly as a consequence.

Reverse Camber The shape of a ski when pressure is applied to its top side and resistance is met at tip and tail. The opposite to normal camber in an unused ski.

Schussing Skis parallel and sliding freely down the flow line.

Slide Slipping Skis travelling more or less sideways, as a consequence of loss of edge grip giving way to the pull of gravity down the slope.

Skidding Skis travelling more or less sideways (relative to their length) as a consequence of being turned at an angle to their original (direction of) motion. May be parallel or ploughing.

Ski Instructor One who instructs skiing – usually holiday-makers, and usually on a short-term basis of up to two weeks (maximum) at one time. Ski instructors usually work in ski schools, and often teach a predetermined sequence of movements or techniques.

Skill A learned ability to select and use appropriate techniques in an efficient manner, in order to achieve an objective or to solve problems or tasks consistently under a wide range of environmental conditions.

Steering The application of pressure against the ski, when that ski is being edged and turned (more or less) at an angle to its motion, causing it to change direction of travel.

Weight The sensation of weight is a consequence of gravity on body mass. Weight acts vertically downwards.

Wellen A similar skiing technique to *avalement* but without the forward projection of the feet. It describes the 'waves' in the terrain over which such a technique would be used.

Index

Other Titles in The Skills of the Game Series

◆ **American Football**	Les Wilson
◆ **Badminton**	Peter Roper
◆ **Basketball**	Paul Stimpson
◆ **Canoeing**	Neil Shave
◆ **Cricket**	Keith Andrew
Cross-Country Skiing	Paddy Field & Tim Walker
◆ **Crown Green Bowls**	Harry Barratt
◆ **Endurance Running**	Norman Brook
◆ **Fitness for Sport**	Rex Hazeldine
◆ **Golf**	John Stirling
◆ **Hockey**	John Cadman
◆ **Judo**	Tony Reay
Jumping	Malcolm Arnold
◆ **Karate**	Vic Charles
Orienteering	Carol McNeill
Rhythmic Gymnastics	Jenny Bott
Rugby League	Maurice Bamford
◆ **Rugby Union**	Barrie Corless
◆ **Sprinting and Hurdling**	Peter Warden
◆ **Squash**	Ian McKenzie
◆ **Swimming**	John Verrier
◆ **Table Tennis**	Gordon Steggall
◆ **Tennis**	Charles Applewhaite & Bill Moss
Throwing	Max Jones
Triathlon	Steve Trew
◆ **Volleyball**	Keith Nicholls
Water Skiing	John West
◆ **Windsurfing**	Ben Oakley

◆ Also available in paperback

Further details of titles available or in preparation can be obtained from the publishers.